FEATHERED FRIENDS

FEATHERED FRIENDS

Ian Niall

CHATTO & WINDUS

THE HOGARTH PRESS

LONDON

Published in 1984 by
Chatto & Windus · The Hogarth Press
40 William IV Street
London WC2N 4DF

British Library Cataloguing in Publication Data
Niall, Ian
Feathered friends.
1. Birds – Great Britain
I. Title
598.2941   QL690.G7
ISBN 0 7011 2772 4

Photoset by Rowland Phototypesetting Ltd
Bury St Edmunds, Suffolk
Printed in Great Britain by
Redwood Burn Ltd
Trowbridge, Wiltshire

CONTENTS

For my grandchildren –
Tom, Anna, Gail, Jamie and Justin

PREFACE

I was born into a world of birds of one sort or another, and they became almost an obsession in my life. I can't say whether, had I been given a choice in the matter, I would ever have had anything to do with keeping fowl, hawks, quail, pheasants, bantams and the like. It wasn't a matter of choice. My grandfather, with whom I started my childhood, had always kept them. Next to horses they were the love of his life. The old man gave me accounts of his experiences and my father added to them, but then I was recruited by my father to be his dogsbody in his aviary, and, when he was on his deathbed, to take over his flock of hens, ducks and geese. I went to live in the house he had lived in. All this is explained in this book. I need hardly say that my days with birds were the happiest of my life.

I am neither a naturalist nor an expert ornithologist. My experience has been practical, but never commercial. I never kept a bird for its eggs or fattened one to put it in a roasting tin. I kept and studied those I did keep because I loved them. I made many mistakes and I may have drawn some wrong conclusions, but this is what happens outside the world of professionals. Foolishly perhaps, I allowed myself that degree of anthropomorphism that makes a severely practical attitude impossible. I know the look in the eye of a creature that trusts me. I always wanted to extend that trust. I really do believe that good intentions can be communicated more easily to most animals than they can to man. I have won over most birds, even if I can't say they all fly to my hand, but then I think I can blame my fellow men for my failures, at least to some extent. I don't expect to be canonised like St Francis, but all life seems sacred to me now. I should have known it long ago.

Some brief explanation of my being on a farm in Galloway, in a

London suburb for a time, and then raising different kinds of birds in Wales is called for perhaps. As a baby I was lucky enough to be sent down from Glasgow to Galloway to be raised by my grandparents. My father, pursuing his career in aeroplane building (he was involved in this industry at the very beginning of the Great War), moved from Glasgow to Middlesex where he was in charge of the drawing office of the Fairey Aviation Company at Hayes. Before the Second World War he went north to Manchester to build a machine called the Battle, Swordfishes and other naval aircraft. He ended his career in Yorkshire where he organised the production of Lancaster Pathfinders. Throughout his life he had been deeply interested in birds of one kind or another, pigeons, canaries, domestic breeds, and in his retirement he settled in North Wales. Quite literally following in his footsteps, I found myself pursuing the same interests. Sometimes I think that, try as we may, some of us can't escape our destinies.

Ashley Green, Buckinghamshire
December 1983

FEATHERED FRIENDS

I THE SCART

My father was old enough to go to school when Grandfather applied for the tenancy of a smithy at Monreith. The family had lived at Garlies-town on the eastern side of the Machars of Wigtown. My aunts-to-be were mere toddlers but father was already a venturesome child and he was delighted with the village of Monreith, a huddle of little stone cottages sheltered from the Luce Bay shore by a mound and sea crags covered with thorns and stunted trees. Below the village was the old kirk which, at that time, was still in regular use and below Kirkmaiden was a sandy bay where waders trilled and stranded fish were sometimes to be found swimming aimlessly round pools across which a boy could comfortably wade. The sound of the sighing sea and the wonderful air made the place paradise that first summer, until, when the harvesters were stooking and thinking what work they might get at potato-picking, Father went to Knock School, up out of the village on the road that undulated along the seaboard to Glaserton and finally, Whithorn. Grandfather had been working for a long time to solve a cultivating problem that would, if he succeeded, enable rows to be scuffled and help in sowing seed in a row. The new smith's inventiveness appealed to the laird's factor and he had put in a good word for him with Sir Herbert Maxwell. Soon however, Grandfather, still working on his scuffler, began to indulge his love of poultry, acquiring pure bred birds, Minorca, Buff Orpington, Wyandote and others. He was a great competitor and was soon taking birds to shows all over Galloway. He did this with the same enthusiasm as his father had had for cock-fighting. When there were no shows coming up he went back to work but all his leisure went into the management of his prize poultry. He soon had a very considerable flock and, since there was no room for them in his cottage garden and the pen he had there, he moved them into the smithy. There they roosted at night, burying their heads in their wings to hide from the glare of the fire and the light of the storm lantern if, as he often did, Grandfather worked on towards the small hours. On fine days the birds wandered along the green, peaceful pathways of the village. They were much more handsome birds than the scrawny fowl kept by the average villager but their condition never pleased their owner and he would give them a shampoo before he took them to shows, especially his White Leghorns who became decidedly sooty roosting above the fire. There were no chicken dinners in this flock. When it came to the eggs the birds laid, once they had been penned for two to three weeks, every egg Grandmother asked for was begrudged. Grandfather always wanted a maximum hatch so that he could cull the most likely chicks for rearing. The rest were sold. If all this was a rather wanton disregard for the proper priorities of a responsible husband Grandmother forgave him. A man doesn't live by bread alone, and she too, was fascinated by the business of breeding and raising livestock.

My father's ambition tended to come of a similar mould. He longed to keep pigeons. He wanted a red-legged 'daw, a chough, if he could find one in the almost inaccessible nooks and crevices in which they nested on the seacliffs at that time. He had to settle for an ordinary jackdaw at first, then a crow and a magpie, but he had plans. His other obsession was with mechanical things, bits of machinery that lay around the smithy in a state of disrepair, anything in fact, that had a driving wheel and a cog. The chaffcutter was not among the discarded bits and pieces but had stood for a long time waiting for its owner to put his hand in his pocket and pay for the welding of some part that had been broken. All it needed, its bearings having become a little stiff, was a squirt of oil. Father had happened to meet an old man in charge of a steam threshing machine who, seeing the boy so taken with machinery, gave him an old oilcan and a lecture on lubricating wheels, hinges, locks and so on. Father was delighted. Everywhere he went he took the oilcan. He oiled the hinges on the school gate. He squirted oil into a neighbour's ear, and he came to the smithy and oiled the chaffcutter. It proved a disastrous exercise, but at first Grandfather praised Father for his usefulness. Oil the wheels and the world rolls on, he said. Leave them to rust and it will all come to a halt, but then it happened. One morning when he came into his smithy he found three of his birds dead on the floor, their feathers bloody, their heads chopped off! Grandfather scratched his own head and wondered if somehow a predator big enough and agile enough to catch a chicken roosting above the floor had slipped in under the door to commit murder. Murder it seemed to be, for although there were feathers around and blood enough, not even the heads had been eaten. Grandfather was still pondering this when he went in for his breakfast that morning. On his return he felt the first raindrops of a shower sweeping over the hillock and leaving a pattern of wet drops on slates and flags. Everyone hurried for cover, including the prize poultry. In out of the rain along with the birds came the village idlers and Father, who wasn't at school that day. The birds picked their way round the feet of the men standing in from the rain, fluffed their feathers, shook themselves and, one after another, flew up to roost until the downpour abated. A wet hen is a sorry sight, however fine it may have looked when it was groomed for the showbench. One of these wet birds flew up into the iron racks. Several of them crowded the area round the chaffcutter. Outside the rain began to pass over until only a drop or two disturbed the newly-formed puddles. Drips fell from the eaves. A breeze shook its own deluge of rain from a bush by the smithy door and then the warm sun set the puddles steaming. The hens perked up, clucked and prepared to flap down to venture out of doors once again. One flapped onto the handle of the recently oiled chaff-cutter and took a downward ride that forced it to spread its wings to maintain its balance. The wheel turned through a full circle as the weight went from the handle and the hen flew onto the floor but this was only the beginning. A second bird, perched with its head close to the wheel, peered through it as the wheel turned and the blade took its head off as fast as the guillotine had taken the heads off its victims in Paris. The cockerel which was decapitated, tumbled to the floor. Its headless body jerked and bounced and somehow recovered its legs. The idlers gasped in amazement. Father's mouth fell open for the now headless cockerel ran through the door and actually turned a corner before it dropped without a kick or a twitch left in it. The idlers called upon God to explain what had happened. They were truly amazed. Like Father, they would talk about it for the rest of their days. Every-one knows that it is the head, even that of a bird-brained creature, that directs the body.

Grandfather dropped his hammer and went to pick up his last remaining prize cockerel. He had won prizes with it. He couldn't have been more upset at the death of a relative and he looked for someone to blame. Who else could he blame but the boy who had oiled the chaffcutter, for before it was oiled it had stood firm as a perching place. It was easy to understand how four birds had been beheaded. Father, for his part was a quick thinking youngster, already far ahead of his father, and went down over the wall and past the old kirk. He stayed there on the shore for most of the day for Grandfather's rage was something to frighten even grown men. Grandmother had already been told of this new disaster. The whole village was agog at the story of a headless bird getting to its feet and running round a corner. It was a kind of miracle. In another place, at another time, a priest would have been summoned to explain it but Grandmother knew the answer. She went out to her potato patch and buried the oilcan. Father came home after climbing walls and struggling through thorns to escape the wilderness down beyond the smithy, for he dared not pass the door of his father's workshop. The sun would be a long time setting on his father's wrath and one of the great treats of Father's young life would cease. He would never be able to accompany his father to the poultry shows again. At these events his friends and his rivals would commiserate with him at being a champion no longer. How could Father and Grandfather look at one another and listen to such words? It was bad enough for Father when his young sisters began to sing 'Who killed Cock Robin?' and chanted 'All the birds of the air fell a sighing and a sobbing!' For several days father and son exchanged no words but then the thing was forgotten. Forty years on, visiting the village of Monreith and the smithy, Father unearthed the rusty remains of the chaffcutter tied to the ground with thongs of briar and bramble. Its owner had never come to redeem it. He had oiled it for nothing, except to be taught that cutting the head off a bird doesn't always make it incapable of getting to its feet and running.

At Knock School Father made friends with the son of a fisherman, a boy called Thomson who liked to climb the crags, poke under rocks for crabs, fish for John Dorys, and rob the nests of the seabirds which were more numerous then than they are now. One day, climbing together the boys came upon a ledge where hungry young cormorants, half-fledged and not as yet able to fend for themselves, stood crowding one another. It occurred to the boys that they could have great fun if they could make a pet of one of these youngsters and train it to fish. The scart, as it is called in that part of the world, is a master fisherman. If the heron sometimes encroaches on the cormorant's preserves and fishes in salt water, he is only a bird of the margins. The scart swims, sleek, smooth and faster than an otter. Its ungainliness when it is on its feet disappears once it goes below. Its paddles propel it along. Its oily feathers mat firmly upon one another until they are like a smooth skin. It sways and glides, and dives. In a matter of seconds it goes through a shoal of fish and catches its dinner. The boys had watched cormorants in deep, clear water hundreds of times, for these fish-hungry birds took fish in the little cove where Thomson's father sometimes set his nets. They were always there in the background to take fish that escaped when the laird's keepers drew their net for the salmon in the mouth of the burn. All the boys needed was a supply of fish to fill the hungry belly of the young cormorant while it grew up, a place to keep it in, and a harness to which they would attach their rope when they took it fishing. This was all a great adventure embarked upon as a result of Father finding a book with drawings of Japanese fishermen using cormorants from their fishing boats. The young scart was housed in an old stone piggery and barricaded in. Each day the boys hunted the shore for fish of one sort or another and carried sea-water with which the young scart was drenched to keep it aware that it was a seabird and neither a pig nor a barnyard fowl. The scart took all they could bring and bolted sandeels, sprats and pollock until its eyes bulged. It stabbed at them when they tried to handle it, however. It looked for more than half a stone of fish a day.

The bird's existence was kept secret from young Thomson's father who, without being aware of the fact, was a contributor to its well-being, for his fish were sometimes stolen before he could get to his nets, while others were 'milked' from the stock he sold round the doors.

Finally a day came when the scart was considered big enough and strong enough to be sent to bring back a mackerel or a Dory. Father, who was very good with his hands, had fashioned a harness to fit the scart and had incorporated in it a swivel to which he fastened the long length of heavy cord to enable him and his friend to drag back both the bird and the fish it caught. The Japanese used a ring round the bird's throat, but Father was content to imagine that he could 'massage' the catch back up the neck of the scart once they had it in their hands again. The day chosen for the trial launch was a lovely one. All along the coast the air was intoxicating. The whole landscape was hazed. Adders basked in the sun. Grasshoppers sang. Yellowhammers sang. Old people sat on their chairs in the doorways of their cottages and slept as soundly as they ever slept in bed. The rocks were hot under their bare feet when they went to put the bird onto the sea after rowing out in Thomson's father's dinghy. Gulls, pursuing sandeels, yelped and screamed and sandeels shot out of the water to escape fish that were after them. Even a young scart entering the water for the first time would quickly decide what it was all about. They checked the scart's harness and its linkage to make sure everything was in working order, pointed the bird in the right direction and encouraged it to go. The bird made a retaliatory stab at them before it flapped onto the clear, blue sea. It dipped its reptilian head into the unusual element of the gentle swell and hung on the harness for a while. It didn't seem to know what to do, but then all at once it dived, towing the line like a hooked pike. They saw the trail of bubbles and the bird seemed to stay an eternity below. They expected it to break the surface with dozens of small fish pouched. It came up, as divers always do, where it was least expected. It stared at them and paddled about to rid itself of the line without success. It didn't seem to have caught a fish. They drew up their anchor and gently paddled after it, thinking it would wait for them and make less disturbance. Could it have been held back in pursuit of the mackerel by the weight of the line? They wondered about this. Maybe it wasn't a day for a cormorant to do well? Free swimming cormorants were far out. Maybe here, in the shelter of the rocks, the water was too still, the black bird too conspicuous for the exercise to succeed, but then sandeels and mackerel broke all round them while the scart sat there on the water looking as though it didn't know what it was supposed to do. The truth was that a scart, like a falconer's bird, doesn't hunt when it is well fed. The boys hauled on the line because the scart had been almost invisibly paddling to keep the same amount of distance between them. The bird came back, flapping and struggling and protesting. They wondered if the wily Japanese had some secret way of making an unwilling cormorant do what it was required to do.

They were in school the following day when Father, his mind wandering from the subject being taught, suddenly cried out 'Too many fish! We need to starve the beggar a bit!' The penalty for disturbing the class was the standard one, a taste of the 'taws' on either palm. Father took his belting and Thomson shouted 'You're right Bob!' Eureka, they had found it! Thomson too, was given a dose of the taws. No one knew what it was all about. The schoolmaster put it all down to a touch of the sun and kept them in that afternoon. They absented themselves a day later. Father fashioned a necklet, hoping to make quite sure that if the scart caught a fish it wouldn't bolt it. They gave their scart no breakfast. They had consulted the book and taken note of the ring the Japanese used, but things were to prove no better on the second occasion. The mackerel weren't there. They waited and drifted close in to the cliff and the rocks at the bottom of it. Suddenly they were accosted by the laird's head keeper who demanded to know what they were up to with the scart. They explained their purpose. The keeper wasn't impressed. He was a mean character constantly at odds with the people of the village over salmon taken with flounder spears as they approached the mouth of the burn, for all fish in the mouth of the burn he deemed the property of his master. Even flounders that were taken in the net used for salmon were not given to the villagers but carted off for the more privileged servants. The boys were overawed but sullenly refused to release the scart so that the keeper could shoot it. He was a man who destroyed everything and anything that could remotely be considered detrimental to the supply of food for the big house or himself. Cormorants, herons, cats and dogs, it made no difference. Although his master was probably unaware of the fact his man was thoroughly detested by his tenants.

Two days later when the boys came to try again the scart took to the water in an encouraging way and seemed to be ready to dive. It did so after a short time spent on the surface and came up with a fish that might have been a John Dory. The boys scrambled to get their small craft moving while the scart, despite the necklet, bolted its prize. By this time they, and the bird, were well under the cliff when there was a startling report from the crag above. The keeper had shot the scart. He didn't bother to come down and retrieve his kill. The dead scart floated, head down, in the water. The boys sorrowfully hauled it in and rowed it away. That evening Father was so grief-stricken he couldn't eat his supper and Grandmother badgered him until he came out with it all. Grandfather heard the story too and was furious. What could he do? Like the other villagers he was only a tenant. The laird's servants, as was often the case in those days, were more powerful and repressive than the landowner himself.

There was something that could be done although it wasn't made plain until the next high tide when the keepers came for the harvest of salmon. They hauled on the net, cursing the small boys who stood 'innocently' trying to pin down a flounder with a bare foot and get away with it, but there seemed to be a snag. The process of drawing the net came to a standstill. The keepers lowered their ropes and waded in, first to their knees, and then beyond their thighs. Everyone had a mental picture of the burn's outflow. Everyone knew there should have been nothing in the way of the net. It took four keepers to remove the thing and they got very wet doing so. The obstruction was an old iron plough and Grandfather was an obvious suspect. He was strong enough to have carried it down from the smithy to the mouth of the burn quite unaided, but the head keeper didn't dare say so. He knew that Grandfather had recently gone into partnership with the laird's agent. There was no way the hard-faced keeper was going to get his own back. The burn was obstructed once again at high tide, but this time the obstruction was more difficult to move. It was a big thorn tree someone had dragged down to the water from the place where it had been growing up at the far end of the village. Two good hauls of salmon lost couldn't have pleased the big house.

2 A BLUE-EYED DUCK

While I was no more than a babe in arms, and barely old enough to
know where I was, I was handed over to my grandparents to be brought
up by them in Galloway where they farmed, Grandfather having sold
up his blacksmith's shop and taken a farm on the proceeds of his
inventions. I wasn't supposed to be long for this world, the way I was
shaping. I couldn't keep my food down. My parents despaired of me
particularly since there was a second child on the way. My sister, who
was born when I was not yet two, contracted sleeping sickness and died
when I was four. Her illness was prolonged and led to my spending
much longer away from home than anyone had anticipated. The result
was that I had a country upbringing in a wonderful world in which the
cock crowed late and early, geese flew in stately flight over the pasture,
peewits called in spring, swooping over their nests on the ploughed
land and the old cart shed was always musical with the twittering of
young swallows that fledged from nests in its rafters. I watched it all
with a childish wonder that has never quite left me. I would be
fascinated to see a starling go in under the eaves and hear the churring

[13]

of its excited young as they waited to be fed. I was often carried to see the waterhen's nest on the broader stretch of water where the ducks swam and the cattle came to drink. It was always built on a flat platform of rock that stood near the far bank of the burn and somehow it remained, even in spate, and the weaving of grass and rushes was never washed away. My grandmother loved to take me to the nest of a wren or a robin, a wagtail or a yellowhammer, and explain to me the different habits of birds. She also, later on, taught me how to snare a rabbit. The sky of those days seems now to have been particularly far up and blue and I trusted everyone. I mistakenly trusted the young leveret that was brought to me to be a pet for, when I went to stroke it, it promptly bit right through my forefinger with those long front teeth hares use when cropping grass. Blood spurted. I cried. I wailed in anguish. The leveret bounded from my arms and quickly loped across the barn floor, squeezed through the door that stood ajar, and went off into the cornfield. I had for the first time experienced that lack of trust my ancestors had induced in wild creatures. I had yet to discover that man to a certain degree destroys almost everything he touches. In a vague way I began to realise, when I was three years old, that there is something lacking in man.

Although the young hare had gone I hankered for a pet of some kind, and my elders, eager to indulge my every whim, took me to a garden fete held on the estate every year between hay and corn harvest. I remember the outcome of that expedition because one of the estate workers had a rabbit hutch for sale, a two-storeyed affair with green algaed timber and a felt roof. There was a sitting tenant in the upper compartment, an over-fed, big black and white buck rabbit. In due course the somewhat rickety hutch with the rabbit inside was carted to the farm and set up by the byre wall. The big rabbit ate enormous quantities of greenstuff, munching away all day and followed dandelion leaves with carrot, meal and tea-leaves. I can't think what the tea-leaves were supposed to do for that great eating machine but I know that the hutch had to be mucked out almost as regularly as the shippon or the stable. The fat rabbit flattened his ears when I stroked him but he was preoccupied with eating and didn't make much of a pet. On reflection I think he may have been infected with tapeworm. The only occasions on which he showed interest were when the door of his 'flat' was opened so that food could be bundled in. If he could have escaped the farm dogs or one of those wild-looking, bull-headed farm cats would almost certainly have had him, big as he was.

I really needed something that would be a companion. The dogs were inclined to shepherd me about, especially if I strayed near the quagmire of the midden. They weren't exactly companions, but one day it was decided I could feed some ducklings newly established in the black shed. The ducklings had been hatched in a wild nest on the far bank of the burn and it was thought they would have a better chance of survival if they were confined for a while. In this mixed brood was one perky little duckling with blue eyes. It twitched its tail and had the kind of character that later on inspired the creator of Donald Duck. It may have been a poor substitute for the pet of my dreams but it tried to converse with me and would detach itself from the others and come to me. I fed it drops of mash. Later on, when the hatch was released and its brothers and sisters bobbed and bounced like small boats in a rough sea as they went over the carts ruts, it would hang back for me and I would toddle after it. Sometimes it would paddle its way on the water round the midden and I would wade after it. On one occasion I lost my boots in the mire. On another my bodyguard of two collies came bouncing in to head me off and the poor duckling scurried off in terror. That duckling knew me.

I have always considered that ducks are far more knowing or intelligent than any other kind of domestic fowl. My blue-eyed duck cultivated me. As a small child I looked at every living creature and expected it to love me and couldn't understand its reluctance to stay with me, but the blue-eyed duckling was obviously a bird apart. It would go into the duck house at night and come out again in the morning, twitching its stumpy tail and preening or looking at the sky before it went to drink. It always seemed to look for me too. When it saw me it would come out of the mud. Everyone smiled to see this, the man harnessing the spring cart, the postman who sometimes came up to the farm with letters, and my aunts who were almost as taken with the bird as I was. One day, however, I came upon Grandfather who had gone to get us a duck for dinner. There he was in the turnip house with his unfortunate victim flapping with its throat cut. I was horrified when I was told that the flesh of a duck has to be drained of blood, like the flesh of a pig, by having blood pumped from its veins as it dies. It was one of the two experiences in my childhood that left a mark on my very soul. (The other was still to come: kissing my grandmother as she lay dead on her bed awaiting the undertaker.) I couldn't really understand why anything as lovely as a duck had to be eaten. I was a child and I grew up to use a gun and kill mallard without thinking what I was doing! I admired the pink roundness of pigs being fattened for the bacon company and their squeals of delight when they jostled round the man who came to put food in their trough. It was surely a world in which there were great contradictions. Wasn't a roast duck one of the loveliest sights you ever saw coming from the oven of the range? I was convinced that the loveliest sight I ever saw was my duck making a bow wave as it swam up the burn or came waddling up the bank to greet me as it often did. They assured me that Grandfather would never kill my duck. It would grow old and die the way people died when they were 'done'. The butcher had to come and kill a lamb or a pig so that we could have fresh meat. The piglets grew to be baconers and the money supplied our needs. This was what a farmer's life was about. There was no time for tears. I was really too young to understand, especially when I found my aunts crying when the bacon company came to collect. That day the squealing was different. The doomed creatures knew what it was all about and we mourned in awful silence after they had gone.

When my parents arrived on a visit from Glasgow I took them to introduce them to my pet. I can remember tugging my mother along by her hand and her protesting that she wasn't properly shod to walk through mud, but she did, looking ruefully at her patent leather shoes when she finally reached the grass of the pasture. To my dismay my duck avoided us. The more we hastened the faster it went bumping on its way. It ignored the titbits I threw to it, kept its head high and hurried on. Mother wasn't convinced that it was a pet. A duck was only a duck to her and this was just another duck. She knew that I was an imaginative child. We went back so that she could have her shoes cleaned and the duck disappeared over a hillock on its way to the burn. My heart was heavy. I thought that something had changed and the duck no longer knew me. I was so despondent about this that my grandmother noticed and gave me some strips of dough from the baking board. 'Go and find your duck,' she said. 'He will come to you if you go by yourself.' I took the trimmings and went off over the field. As I approached the water the duck, who had been sifting black mud with its neck outstretched, stopped what it was doing and paddled to the bank, hurrying to meet me. I knew then what it was about. A good shepherd knows his sheep, the Bible says, but this isn't just a biblical truth. A shepherd actually knows the different faces of his flock and the relationship between man and animal is personal, individual, and hardly ever broadly shared. The duck knew and trusted me. It didn't know my mother in a long black dress and with a hat on her head. I had visited it every day and it had come to look for me, outside the duck shed, along the midden side, or down by the water. I sought its company whenever I could but sometimes a downpour that delighted the ducks kept me indoors. The ducks would tack to and fro on the flood of the burn picking morsels from the fast flowing water while the rain teemed down; I stayed indoors and the downpour beat on the skylights. Even when the rain fell unabated all day I would watch for the return of the ducks from the burn. There were no foxes for miles, but there were half-wild dogs that ranged far and wide and those feral cats that haunted the rickyard, to say nothing of the stoat or the whitterick that changed to white in winter. Willie, the byre boy, had lost a monster polecat ferret almost the size of an otter they said, and they blamed this beast for taking a hen every now and again.

I hadn't noticed that my beloved pet had outgrown me. It was already out of its adolescence while I was still a child. It was laying an egg or two, sometimes on the watercourse where the egg would sink into the peaty silt and sometimes on the bank of the burn. My aunts always went down to scoop these eggs from the water and search for others on the bank, but ducks, like wayward hens, find secret places to lay and hatch a clutch undetected. One bright morning they are found back on the water with a whole flotilla of tiny ducklings behind them desperately trying to swim against the current. When this happened the brood would be shepherded off the water and on up the field to the steading. Here they would find quarters in the black shed to save them from the attention of predators and the cold nights of early summer. 'Look,' my aunts would say each year, 'Ten little ducks saved from the whittericks and the rats!' Black rats lived along the burn at that time, a hangover perhaps, from a day when they were the common sort of rat found in Britain, but the grey rat swarmed through the rickbutts in the stackyard and they weren't particular what they ate, a chick or a duckling.

The peewits had nested that spring and soon after partridges were laying in nests on the side of the old road to what we called the switchback hills. In maybe three or four weeks young partridges would be making dustbaths on the spoil of molehills, and running, when they were disturbed, into the minor forests of turnip field weeds. It was at this time that I missed my pet. She hadn't come back from the burn that evening. I couldn't get to sleep for worrying in case some harm might have befallen her. They told me she must be laying away and had gone to sleep in the nest in the briars the way a duck sometimes does. In the morning I asked my aunts to come and help me search for her but they were busy scalding cans in the dairy and finishing their urgent chores. The blue-eyed duck, they assured me, would come to no harm. She was safe and sound in the cover of grass and blackberry and when she had a mind to come to be fed she would come up to the steading. If need be they would take one of the dogs and he would mark the nest for them. My duck would come home like Little Bopeep's sheep. I went down to the burn and called my duck and scattered titbits on the water which the rest of her brothers and sisters quickly bolted down. I was more anxious than ever for who was to say a fox hadn't come down from those blue, far-off hills to hunt along the burnside? Grandfather said they sometimes did venture into the keeper's domain just as the deer came down in winter to raid the rootfield or browse on sheaves along the side of the stackyard.

In the afternoon the younger of my two aunts brought her crook to search the brambles on the bank and, if need be, the out-lying clumps of whins. She was quite convinced we would find my duck, and at last we did. There she was under cover of greenery sheltering in a coil of old rusty fencewire in which she had made her nest. Right in the middle sat my cream-coloured, blue-eyed duck, but her head hung limply on her breast. All round her were those downy feathers she had plucked from herself to line her nest so that when she waddled off to take a drink or get something to eat her eggs would still be warm. She had been bitten in the neck, falling victim, Grandfather decided, to an otter that had come up the burn as they sometimes did at this time of year, for here and there in the burn there were trout to be taken as well as young birds. The summer sun had darkened for me. The world would never be the same again. I had never even seen an otter and in fact didn't see one at close quarters until I was a grown man. The keeper must have spotted the otter's tracks along the burn somewhere, however. Perhaps he detected its presence where it left the remains of a trout and set a trap for it. In due course the otter stepped into the gin set cunningly under water and was anchored there until the time came for the man who had trapped it to collect it. He didn't come in time, it turned out. Instead, a neighbour of ours, wandering along the burn's course, found the otter and took it away to have it stuffed. I was older and over the sadness of losing my duck when we visited that neighbour. There, in a glass case on the sideboard, the otter stood, mounted on a rock and with a fish between his forepaws. He was without doubt the murderer of my blue-eyed duck but somehow I took no satisfaction from seeing him there, his fangs bared and his head inclined to take a bite from that stuffed fish. Mine was a different kind of sadness. It was for all the world, the duck, the otter, the man who set the trap, as well as myself, and it had a profound effect upon me much much later on in life.

3 DANNY AND THE PEACOCK

Vanity in humans is generally treated with amusement or scorn, but I am not sure that a peacock really deserves to be dubbed a vain bird when it is only doing what is natural for it to do. Regard the bird anthropomorphically however, and it may be called other things than simply vain – self-important, conceited, class-conscious, even arrogant. Peacocks have always fascinated me because I almost owned one for seven days, but, I hasten to say, mine wasn't a particularly grand bird, and it had to be returned to the park in which it rightfully belonged. A piggery is no place for a peacock, and even if it had been in a fit state to spread its tail and strut on the field, it wouldn't have looked very special steering its way through nettles and yellow ragwort at the back of the high barn. I wouldn't have had this bird at all but for Danny.

Danny came to work for my grandfather after serving in the war. Whether he had been much of a soldier or not I don't know, but he had a word tattooed on his forearm that suggested he hadn't been. The word was Barlinnie which was/is a pretty infamous prison. I was too young to be able to read the word, and Danny, I was told long afterwards, couldn't read it himself. It seemed that once, when he was very drunk, the soldiers he was with hauled him into a booth and paid to have the name of the prison etched on his arm. Afterwards they told him it was his own Christian name. When he found out it wasn't he would work with his shirt sleeves rolled down even on the hottest of harvest days. The word came to have significance, for Danny was often in the hands of the police. They could read, but it never seemed to strike them that a really dedicated criminal would never have had Barlinnie put on his arm. They pushed Danny about a lot and he might as well have had the word put on his forehead. When he came to work at the farm he took to me because I listened to what he had to say. Nobody else did. He was a sturdy little man, past middle age and unmarried. He had lost both parents when the house they were living in burned down. Thereafter he was brought up by his mother's sister. She still looked after him, even when he came back from the war, and he took his washing back to her every other week-end when he had a day and a night off. Danny loved birds and I loved them too. Whenever the opportunity presented itself he would take me to watch the swallows as they flitted in and out of the cart shed where they nested on the beams. We watched the waterhen walking on the ooze beyond the byre midden and more than once ran to catch a second glimpse of the corncrake that would cross the wee field, the home paddock behind the steading, to get to the hayfield beyond. There was, I am sure, a particular innocence about Danny that hardly anyone else appreciated.

The peacock catastrophe came upon us when, one weekend as he was tying his washing on his battered bike, Danny looked at me and winked and said, 'I'm going to get you a peacock, son, but you'll promise not to say a word?' I promised. I knew what a peacock was for not long before I had watched peacocks on a lawn. They seemed to me to be like my Great Aunt Ellen who never walked but glided on castors that were hidden under her long dress. Like her, they were grand, far above other birds like turkeys or geese, who held their heads high and couldn't be persuaded to retreat once they decided they would hold their ground. Great Aunt Ellen was a ladies' companion, which meant she was far above a mere white-gloved flunkey. Even the butler, with the key to the port in his waistcoat pocket, deferred to Her Ladyship's companion, and why shouldn't he when she and her mistress conversed in French while they sat with their embroidery? Once a year, however, Her Ladyship went off to visit cousins and Great Aunt Ellen was left to hold sway if not in the mansion itself, in her grace-and-favour cottage in the grounds, and on the lawns, when she chose to stroll there, giving herself airs as though her family tree went all the way back to Eve. Once a year my grandparents were invited to visit the estate and stay with Great Aunt Ellen, but Grandfather contrived to have urgent tasks to perform. He was too frustrated by those minuscule sandwiches his sister-in-law served and always in danger of breaking the eggshell teacups in his enormous, horny hands. In consequence, on this particular occasion I was taken as a stand-in. I was well-behaved. I ate the sandwiches and broke none of the teacups, and as a reward I was taken to see the peacocks. To tell the truth I have never since seen peacocks like them. They paraded. They turned their magnificent emerald-eyed tails this way and that. They bedazzled me. It seemed to me that they must belong to a king. No one else could possibly own one, even the laird with his brass-lamped motorcar and his ear-flapped tweed bonnet could hardly aspire to owning anything so magnificent. When Danny told me he would get me one I only half believed him. Grandfather had promised me a merry-go-round and it had turned out to be a cartwheel that rotated on a crowbar driven into the ground. The peacock was another of our joint flights of fancy. We often flew with the heron when it took off from the burnside or sailed with that high-up eagle that soared on sunny afternoons above the distant Galloway hills. I really didn't understand that Danny, whose elderly aunt lived on another estate where peacocks ranged, was determined to steal one and bring it to the farm in a sack when he returned on Sunday evening. Such folly could never have been contemplated by the true 'criminal' and one with Barlinnie on his forearm! Danny, I can see now, was a case of arrested development while I was a child who was used to magic, an owl on my bedrail and a duck that talked to me.

It must have been quite dark when Danny brought the peacock or even he would have expected to have been apprehended before he had gone a mile. Somehow he managed to wheel his bicycle along the road. He coped with the unhappy bird in the sack that badly damaged its tail and with its crowning glory, the top-knot of feathers which a male peacock has to go with the rest of its magnificent plumage. There was no one sitting up to see Danny arrive. He safely made his way to the piggery at the back of the high barn and released the prize into the sty, closing the door and covering the yard with wire-netting he had laid close by for that purpose. The peacock probably crouched where it dropped until daybreak, altogether terrified by its ordeal. No one went to the old piggery except once in a blue moon when hens were laying in the wild and there was a fall in egg production. It seemed the only place in which the stolen bird could be safely housed. How it would be explained when, in due course its presence was revealed, Danny couldn't have thought about. Peacocks don't arrive as an act of God and it couldn't possibly have flown or walked from the nearest estate that kept such birds. Someone must have brought it. Danny was the natural suspect but this was something else he hadn't considered. Thief was branded upon him. He might as well have carried the word on his discharge papers. He had to expect retribution sooner or later. The peacock was not, so soon after its traumatic move, in any mood to shriek the way peacocks on lawns do but it would find a way of letting its presence be known, given the slightest opportunity. Danny winked at me that morning when I was brought out, washed, dressed and my hair combed, so that I could accompany Grandfather to the creamery with the milk.

'I got a bird to show you,' Danny said, smiling happily.

I had to get up on the spring cart beside Grandfather. This was one of my special treats. When the milk churns were unloaded and empties put in their place we would turn aside at the bridge over the Bladnoch and trundle up the village street to a little shop that sold sweets and almost everything else you could think of. Grandfather would buy his ounce of black twist and a bag of sweets, after which we would jog home to the accompaniment of the jangling churns while Grandfather smoked his rank tobacco and I gorged on dolly mixtures. This was a great Monday morning event, one I only missed when the weather was bitterly cold. Even when it lashed with rain I went to the creamery for I had a fine set of oilskins that made me look like a miniature deep sea fisherman straight from a Scott's Emulsion advertisement. I remember this particular jaunt because Danny still hung about the steading to see me when he should have been away down in the bog field cutting thistles. As soon as I could slip away I hurried to meet him. He positively hauled me round to the old piggery and hoisted me onto the gate to see the peacock, but it was all a bit of a let-down. The peacock was a very dejected bird. Its tail feathers were covered in fragments of straw from the pigs' bedding. It didn't seem in the least inclined to come out into the sunlight and it looked much smaller with its tail down. Some of its quills were broken like barley stalks after a high wind.

'It's not as big as a turkey,' I remember saying.

'It's tail will grow better,' Danny assured me. 'It'll soon be like itself again. It's not at home here yet, but it will be.'

It was never going to be at home. It was used to better things: first-class accommodation, grander surroundings, respect. Our secret delighted me for all of three days during which I would sneak off to stand on tip-toe, peer into the sty and try to make friends with the peacock. The peacock only skulked or sulked and when Danny came along it got hysterical. There was nothing he could do to calm its nerves. It had a terrifying recollection of being grabbed by the neck and thrust into a dirty sack. I can only speculate about the way Danny must have stalked it on the fringe of a lawn and rushed after it to capture it in the cover of rhododendrons and azaleas. It had probably shrieked more than once and caused panic among its companions. If there was a regular headcount of birds the keeper would have started looking for evidence of the presence of a fox, or the intrusion of some ravenous, stray dog. After that he would have talked to the policeman and the policeman would have rubbed his chin and thought of Danny. All this is hindsight long delayed. At the time I was too young to work such things out, too innocent to appreciate that I was involved in a criminal act. Here, for the time being, was a bird in a cage, living in a hovel from which it was soon to escape and make itself known by taking wing. Unlike the cockerel in Will Waterproof's lament, it wouldn't fly in grand style across the Home Counties and end up as a golden sign for a city chophouse. It would struggle out from beneath the chicken wire and the poles holding it down, flutter onto the sloping roof of the piggery, fly from the moss-covered slates to reach the roof of the high barn, and perch there on the ridge, putting the pigeon strays to flight. My aunts would see it there and they certainly did.

'Dear Lord,' they said, 'do you see what is up there on the roof?'

I said I did see, but I couldn't say how it got there for I had solemnly sworn not to divulge our secret.

My aunts agreed with one another. It was a peacock, but a poor looking bird and nothing to be compared with the birds they had seen gliding on a lawn beyond a ha-ha, those male mannequins of the bird world, bird aristocrats that adorned the private park and were the only creatures, other than doves, that broke a cathedral silence. My aunts were not slow when it came to deduction. Sherlock Holmes might have told them it was elementary, but in no time at all they had nominated Danny. Did I know anything about it? At this period in my young life I was said to have such innocence that I was simply born to be a minister! Even the Minister himself, when he called to have tea and demolished the shortbread, agreed that I already looked a most likely candidate for the cloth. I didn't know how the peacock got there, I said. I was telling the truth. I couldn't imagine how Danny had managed it. I certainly didn't know how the peacock had got out of the pigsty and flown onto the ridge. Danny was beyond redemption, they said. Wickedness was in him! He had stolen the bird from the estate on which his poor old auntie lived. Not only would he be sent away to prison, 'put in the "jile"' they called it, but his auntie would probably be banished from the estate, turned out without a penny to bless herself! It was at this stage of their speculation that Grandfather arrived on the scene. He stumped down the steading and stood gazing at the phenomenon. What in God's name was a peacock doing there? He was aghast when it came to him, the obvious answer. He not only recognized a crime. He knew who owned the bird. The sooner it was captured and returned the better! This was easier said than done. The peacock seemed determined to stay out of harm's way. It managed to do so for a whole day, but at evening it finally came off the ridge, slipping and sliding down the slope of the slates and finally flapping into the yard.

Not a word of recrimination had been directed at poor Danny. It went without saying. Danny, sent to Coventry and with nothing to say for himself, must have thought I had 'told on him'. He had been on sentry go all day. When the bird came down he rushed it into a corner and for a second time grabbed it by the neck. The captive was put in a barrel. It was too late to transport it back to that world of yews, cedars and immaculately kept lawns, but on the following morning Grandfather dressed himself in his best suit, put on his bowler hat and had the gig yoked to his trotting pony. As a treat (the second treat of the week!) I was allowed to go along. We rode in silence most of the way. There wasn't very much that could be said on my side and Grandfather was probably rehearsing what he would say to the owner of the bird with whom he had had dealings in the past. This connection proved fortunate indeed for, once he was past the self-important head-gardener and the keeper, Grandfather was able to smooth everything over. There was no question of Danny's auntie being evicted or being held responsible for the crime. Danny was entirely to blame. I heard Grandfather saying he would give him a raging and send him off down the road. He couldn't think what had made him do such a thing. I could. He had done it to delight me. He would have done anything for me.

Danny wasn't there to take the tongue lashing. As soon as Grandfather departed with the peacock he had hurried in to get his bundle of clothes and tie it on his bicycle. He didn't stop even for a bowl of broth, but rode away, steadily heading for the blue distance of the far moss and the other side of the shire. I never saw him again but I have never forgotten him.

4 THE STORY OF JOE THE RAVEN

The raven's saga runs through a good part of my life for a raven was
among my earliest memories. I have written about it at different times
and told how I first made its acquaintance. The raven of my adolescence was another bird, owned by the son of the blacksmith who first
took me fishing, and it might well have been that raven who plagued the
children on their way to the country school when I was a small child
myself. The fact that that world of more than sixty years ago was a
well-keepered one meant that we saw few predatory birds, fewer hawks
and falcons certainly, and not many magpies although the crow was
always there. If the crow saw a man crossing a field, whether with a gun
or without one, it veered away. We never saw a buzzard. If there had
been any they had all, long since, been killed off. Even the handsome
long-eared owl that haunted the conifers on the edge of the moss would
be shot. We did see eagles once in a long while, sailing on the upcurrent
of winds above the Galloway hills. The raven was to be seen on sea
crags but more often confined itself to the wilderness of hill country
and moorland. It never ventured across the pastureland or the arable

fields of the Machars. When I was quite small I used to wander down from the farm to the blacksmith's shop a mile or so away. Everything about the smithy fascinated me, the volcano of the fire, the way white hot iron was beaten into new shapes, the way the smith, Willie Adair, spat tobacco juice to frighten a dog, for he could launch a shaft of brown juice like a spear with unerring aim to hit a dog three or four yards away. This delighted onlookers who sometimes were themselves forced to get out of the way when the smith wanted room in which to manipulate a piece of long, glowing iron. Stray dogs went off with their tails between their legs and the idlers fell back upon one another or had their boots spattered by the smith's expectorated cud-chewings. This world was one in which strong language and blasphemy were commonplace. When I was no more than five years old there was nothing I didn't know about the nature of man or woman. All I had done was to keep my eyes and my ears open, like the raven the smith took as his mascot.

Some time before I began to visit him the smith acquired a raven from a family of itinerant tinkers. These wild people had come down from the hills of Ayrshire or somewhere like that, bringing with them a hollow-backed pony that trotted behind, three whippets and the raven in a makeshift cage. The bird, I was told later in life, had been taken from a nest somewhere in the wilderness to be traded for anything acceptable. Willie Adair put shoes on their pony, watched that they didn't steal his iron or any of his bantams, and accepted the bird along with a whippet in payment for his work. He bartered and haggled with them over the whippet and said he had no use for their bloody crow but to tell the truth it was the crow he wanted and when they left he took the bird from its cage of split hazel and cropped one of its wings as he sometimes cropped the wing of one of his bantams so that it wouldn't fly off. In a few days he was sharing his 'piece' with the black bird and the bird was getting used to the smoke and fume and flying sparks of the smithy. Soon the raven learned that fire burns and ceased to get his feathers singed. He also learned the language of the smith while he roosted up under the rafters. Willie's curses were always colourful but when he cursed the bird his words were really a kind of endearment and he wouldn't have parted with it for all the money in the world. It was his alter ego, as black as he was and in need of company. The big kee-aw (all members of the crow tribe, carrion crow or rook, were known as kee-aws) wasn't conspicuous in the dark recesses of the smithy unless one looked closely, and there it sat, sometimes with its pickaxe of a bill in its wing and sometimes contemplatively watching the fire. It would have been just an ornament about the place but for its character. The smith had more cats and dogs and bantams than any one man might have needed and I was unaware that he had a kee-aw of any kind, but one day as I approached the smithy a gruff, guttural voice said, 'Hello Joe! Hello Joe!'. I knew the voice for it was the smith's, although he was at that moment down in the burn quenching iron. It seemed someone was playing a prank on me. I looked about and saw the outsized crow, a very tattered looking bird, perched on the drystone wall above my head. I knew that magpies could be made to talk if their tongues were split but I had never heard one talking. A second cousin of my aunts who had gone to sea had long promised to bring back a talking parrot but he had never done so. Instead he had married an unhandsome lady who talked more than any parrot. The raven looked down at me as though expecting some reward. When I moved on he flapped down from the wall and came scuttling after me but I ran to escape his attentions. The smith was back inside the smithy when I got there and he grinned when I told him the crow had said hello. He picked up a small stone and hurled it at his bird which had appeared in the doorway, and the raven skipped into the air and dodged the missile. 'He's an old black bastard, that's all he is!' he told me. I didn't know it but the smith was teaching the bird this phrase, making it into a kind of personal jester. It could already give a perfect imitation of its master saying, 'Stand still damn ye!' and 'Had up!', commands the smith often used to the horses in for shoeing. The bird's vocabulary grew because for the greater part of his day the smith had no one to talk to. The dogs were turned out, not by the smith, but by the raven itself, which would rush after them to deliver blows with its beak, swearing like the smith. I suppose it was the guttural voice that made these animals run. The bird's reputation spread far and wide and people came to hear it swear in its master's voice, but then it began to express its own character. It chased the children as they came and went from the country schoolhouse beyond the bridge. It pecked their bare legs and wore out its pinioned wing, using it as a kind of crutch as it rushed after them muttering, 'God damn ye!' Boys and girls jumped over walls and across ditches to escape and in time the raven was able to give a fair imitation of their squeals of anguish. A few of the braver boys might stop to pick up a stone and throw it at the black bird, but the raven was highly practised in dodging and swore at them again. Rarely did one of the boys try to stand his ground and aim a kick at his persecutor, but when he did the raven would ride with the boot and flap onto the wall. All that happened would be the loss of a black feather. The raven was neither hurt nor intimidated.

The smith was well aware that his bird was becoming a great nuisance but he took a certain delight in this and shrugged his shoulders when the grey-haired old school mistress came over the bridge to protest, telling him the language of the bird was a disgrace and she knew where he got it from! Not only was it a cursing nuisance but it inflicted wounds on boys and girls. Unless it stopped she would have the policeman brought to wring the bird's neck. 'I am not responsible, mistress!' the smith told her. 'It is a free bird and your boys stone him. He knows what to do to look after himself! Send their fathers to see me and I'll have a few words for them, you can be sure of that.' I remember being there when this encounter took place. I was completely overawed by it all. When it was over Willie picked up a rusty bolt and threw it at the bird. The raven let it pass under him and swore, but he somehow reminded me of the preacher who came on a Sunday evening to the schoolhouse breathing fire and brimstone. The raven's eye was as bright as the evangelist's although what he had to say was somewhat less reverent.

'Yon raven is a disgrace just the same,' my aunts said, 'teaching the children bad words!' Indeed the raven not only taught the children how to swear with emphasis but controlled a whole stretch of road, belonging there like the stone breaker who sat in the quarry making material for filling potholes or Soldier Scott who marched up and down yet another stretch of country road, saluting and standing to attention when anyone came past. Joe, the raven, had a disturbing habit of hopping up on a wall and scaring not only children but sometimes adults who fell off their bicycles, grazing hands and knees when he greeted them with guttural curses. I spent a lot of my time watching the bird and its master. They fascinated me. Their rapport depended, it seems to me now, on mischief. Willie delighted in the scenes the bird created. 'I'll kill that bloody bird!' he would exclaim when it limed him from a perch above his metal store. 'I'll put the bugger on the fire!' The raven would echo, 'bugger on the fire!' but everyone knew it would never happen. Willie loved the bird. It was like a son to him, Grandfather said, smiling in his beard. For some reason I was one child the raven didn't plague but perhaps this was because I learned to keep a titbit in my pocket, bits of egg-yolked crust Grandfather sometimes left on the side of his plate. Joe seemed to look at me with a knowing eye. This may or may not be anthropomorphism but when he came towards me, using that worn down wing tip as a crutch, he reminded me of a one-legged soldier to whom Grandfather often threw a shilling. Willie's raven was a kind of a beggar too and he hung around until he had the last crust from my pocket. He somehow knew when I had no more to offer and went off about his business but I was never molested as the children who went to the school were. Maybe if they had thought to give him a bit of their piece he would have let them pass, but they never did, and he remained their scourge while they were in short trousers. 'He kens ye,' the smith said. 'It's them he disna ken he dabs.' I was glad he 'kenned' me better than other children.

Time and circumstances bring about changes in everything. I grew up without Joe rather than with him, for I was taken off to live with my parents in Glasgow and returned to my Grandfather's mostly in school holidays. When the smith took me fishing, when I was perhaps eight years old, and I was still in short trousers, I encountered Joe on the road but he let me pass without pecking my bare legs. He may have come to see if I had aught to offer in the cause of charity. By all accounts he himself was by no means poor and penniless, for he readily accepted copper coins, generally a penny which he would put on one side while he pecked a hole in the ground to hide it in. This done, he would put the penny in the hole and pick up a small stone which he not only covered it with, but drove home with his beak. If anyone watched him too closely he would simply carry the penny off and bury it somewhere else. People would give him coins to see him do this. 'He's just's a bloody miser,' the smith told me. 'He has money hidden all over the place. He doesn't know how much he's worth, but maybe he digs it up and puts it all in a bigger hole somewhere for his old age. He's like my old grandfather who was always hiding money somewhere.' Some of the loungers would poke about with a stick hoping to find Joe's hoard but as far as I know they never found a penny of it, and there may have been something in what the smith said.

Old Willie and I fished the burn with spruce pole rods, brown line and hooks to gut after we had dug worms either from his midden by the smithy or from his garden. Joe came with us and hung about in the hope of getting a worm thrown to him but worms were precious. On the right day each one meant a trout from a pool in flood and we put them in moss in a jam jar and left the bird to his own resources. It was easy fishing. The spruce pole would bend, the line cut water and the hook would be set in a good brown trout. Once I remember I caught ninety. Most of them went to feed the hens but almost every time I went I would encounter Joe on my way past the smithy. He waited for a fish which he didn't eat but buried, doing the same thing with it that he did with a penny, making a hole and burying it. Perhaps he liked his carion meat a little high and dug it up later. The smith would cook fish on his burnished shovel and swore that it was the perfect way to cook a trout, for gutting the fish released unsavoury juices from the intestine to contaminate the meat. Joe would be thrown a cooked trout and he knew to leave it for a while until it cooled.

Joe and I were contemporaries but of course he has been dead long since and I did not witness his end. After I mentioned him in a book, some years after I knew him, a friend went to find the smithy and see if Joe was still around, but alas Old Willie had gone to tend another fire without an anvil or a bit of iron to be forged. Young Willie had taken his place and recalled Joe telling the world, 'I'm an old black bastard, that's all I am!' which is probably the longest sentence a raven or any bird like it has ever been taught to say. There was another raven at the smithy, a silent replica of Joe who couldn't have plagued the boys by pecking their knees, even if the house on the other side of the bridge hadn't been converted from a school to a country library, because the boys would have been conforming to fashion and wearing jeans. There were no Sunday preaching meetings. Religion too, had gone out of fashion. The new raven sat watching cars speeding past without so much as a curse. It didn't, as far as I am aware, get a penny from a passer-by let alone a trout from the burn. Despite the pace of the world and the fumes of petrol polluting the countryside it may live to a greater age than its predecessor. Joe wasn't equipped for the modern world.

One day he failed to flap out of the way and was killed by a passing car, bowled over in a flurry of black feathers and left lying on the road, flapping until his life was spent. Like his master he was a character.

5 OWLS ON THE CHIMNEY

Even as a small child I was quite without fear of the dark. In fact, then, as now, I took comfort in it, and when I blew out my candle and the shadow rushed in upon me I found it as snug as a blanket. I usually slept upstairs but when someone was unwell and my sleep was likely to be disturbed I was put downstairs in what was designated my parents' bedroom, even although they only used it on infrequent visits. I slept down there in an enormous, enveloping bed with a chaff mattress, the healthiest kind of bed ever invented, and one calculated to induce sleep quicker than a hop pillow. The bed itself had a towering, quilted bed head and a similarly quilted bed end which I could barely see over. On nights when there was a moon the small room, crowded by the bed, a massive mahogany wardrobe three or four men could have stood in, and a large dresser with the usual large bowl and waterjug, was bathed in soft, eerie light. On warm nights the window would be lowered to let in the scents of honeysuckle and tea rose growing by the porch. I loved it in summer when I could lie in bed and breathe the scent of the hayfield where the mower had been to cut clover and ryegrass. When I

[37]

had had a little too many scones and bits of shortbread for supper I sometimes didn't manage to fall asleep, in spite of the soporific scent of chaff and the perfume of honeysuckle, and I would lie and listen to the small sounds of the night: the subdued murmur from the kitchen where my aunts sat by the fire darning a sock or knitting while they drank yet another cup of weak tea, the far-off lowing of cattle or the occasional barking of a dog.

On one particular night when I lay awake long after my aunts had gone up the creaky stairs to their bedroom, I watched the moon, like an enormous florin slowly moving across the sky, and all at once I heard a peculiar, hissing sound. I knew the cries of the night, even the squeak of a mouse or the squeal of a rat, but this was different, and it was close at hand. I climbed down out of bed and went across the cold wax-cloth to the open window to peer out. There was nothing I hadn't seen before: whitewashed walls, black shadows by the porch. A gentle breeze made the lace curtains billow. Finally I tiptoed into the hall and turned the handle of the porch door, a door no one ever bothered to lock. The door itself was as good as an alarm for it had complaining hinges and it grated along the floor when it was opened. I squeezed through and stood on pebbles brought from the shore to make a pathway round the house. There was nothing out of the ordinary. The windows glinted in the moonlight the way Great Aunt Ellen's glasses seemed to glint when she seemed to be looking nowhere. The skylights were like shining mirrors on the blue-black slates. There wasn't even a trickle of smoke from the chimneys. I looked up at those rather squat stone chimney stacks. On the western gable-end, right on the edge of the stack, sat three white owls no bigger than fantail pigeons. I stared up at them and they seemed to be staring down at me. I don't think I have ever seen anything so enchanting as those newly-fledged owlets. Time must have stood still until I became aware of the chill of pebbles under my feet and the flannel of my nightshirt being moulded to my legs by the breeze. The clock chimed inside the farmhouse. It made a sound I never forget, for it had a particularly light, brassy note that not every long-case, chiming clock makes. I was about to get back indoors when, without a sound, one of the adult birds came over the chimney stack, sailed silently in a circle and dropped what appeared to be a mouse onto the stack. Almost at once the three owlets disappeared down the chimney. Their parent sailed on out over the moonlit field and turned to hunt round the steading and the rickyard beyond. I listened to the commotion in the chimney. The young owls were battling over their supper. When they had devoured it they would come back up into the moonlight and hiss to draw attention to their need for more. It was magical and my world had increased in dimension. I hadn't known before that owls were nesting in the chimney in some recess, just out of the peat reek, perhaps, but birds that are mainly nocturnal can escape notice. I must have been lost in a dream for I was startled to find someone there in the dark entry. 'God's sake, boy, what are you doing out here in the middle of the night?' my aunt demanded. I almost jumped out of my skin. A protective arm was put round my shoulder. I was petted and pacified quite unnecessarily. They must have thought I had been sleep-walking.

'There are owls living in our chimney!' I said. 'I heard them making a noise like an angry goose!' but my aunt seemed to know all about it. 'Never you mind about the hoolerts,' she said. 'Get back into your warm bed now. What your grandfather would say I don't know!' I got back into bed and in a short time I was asleep. The following morning everyone was too busy to talk about owls, but I managed to way-lay Grandmother. She said there were ledges in the chimney plenty big enough for a family of owls. It was a lucky house that had birds nesting under its roof or in its chimney, and I should remember that. There was always a curse put on anyone who drove them away or destroyed their nests. My grandmother was well up in country lore and she believed that a crow flying directly over the roof, or perching on it, was an omen of death. If the crow flew directly over the house one of our relatives was near to death. If it perched someone in the house would die, and she worried about this sort of thing until she made enquiries about all of our immediate kinfolk. The owls, my grandfather told me later, were a godsend to us for they killed mice and voles. Mice ruined the ricks and voles undermined good pasture, spoiling it the way moles did. The owls kept down mice, voles, and rats if they came across young ones, so they were never to be driven off or discouraged.

No fires had been lit in the down-the-house room for weeks because my grandfather had guessed the owl was incubating. Now the young were up on the stack it wouldn't be long before the whole family of them started hunting, taking hundreds of mice and saving bushels of corn. I was persuaded that the owls liked living with us. In return for warmth and shelter they kept the mice down. It was a fairy tale come true. Soon after this, while I was still in the downstairs bedroom, an even more surprising thing happened. I had had no idea that there was a fireplace in the bedroom for the whole area of wall at that end of it was covered by the enormous mahogany wardrobe. My grandmother hadn't been able to resist massive furniture when they came to the farm, and my grandfather had indulged his own passion for bidding at sales by buying her huge items in mahogany sold up when the equivalent of a baronial hall came under the hammer. One day the great wardrobe was levered away from the wall and there, to my surprise, was one of those ancient cast iron fireplaces with a narrow iron mantelshelf. I don't suppose the fire had been lit for a hundred years. The hearth and firebasket were full of sticks and other debris tumbled down the chimney. Before the owls there may have been a generation or two of jackdaws or birds like starlings, and perhaps the battling of the owlets had brought the nest material down. My aunts were delighted to have the opportunity of a spring clean even in summer. They blamed the owls for the mess, although the barn owl doesn't make a nest and lays on any suitable ledge out of direct light whether in the roof of a barn or a chimney stack. Fussing over their cleaning my aunts even found a papered-over cupboard in the chimney-breast, but when they opened it it didn't reveal the owls, as I had hoped. The only thing it contained was a pencil fashioned from the bullet and cartridge case of a single round of rifle ammunition brought back, perhaps, by someone who had been at the Boer War. My aunts' cleaning was interrupted for several days by the urgent need to get hay in before the corn harvest and this led to a much closer encounter with the owls.

The brood in the chimney seemed to snooze all day and become active just at twilight when their parents went off across the fields on their nightlong excursions to find food. I could tell when the adult birds were coming in for the hissing always became more and more pronounced. At first it might come from deep inside the chimney where, in the darkness, the old stone flues divided, but finally the young birds flapped and fluttered to the top and hissed furiously to tell their parents to be quick about it and bring them bigger and better things. I always fell asleep without discovering whether the noise went on until morning or died away as the well-fed young owls retired to digest the food they had so greedily gobbled down. One night, however, I found myself awakened by a disturbance in the chimney. The hissing had begun again and it was clearer than ever before. I stared across the room in the direction of the fireplace, which I couldn't see because it was out of the line of my vision, obscured by the wardrobe now only a foot from the bed end. To my amazement I saw three owlets. One of them turned and looked back at me from his perch on the bed end. His companion ignored me. The third owlet made a silent flit from the end of the bed to the waterjug and took wing again to fly round as silently as a butterfly. Only a fly dropping on butter moves so perfectly inaudibly. The bird facing me was suddenly airborne too. Only one remained now and I heard the other two fluttering in the chimney. I wasn't in the least alarmed to have an owl sitting there, its head completely twisted round the wrong way as it kept me in view but I wanted someone else to see what I had seen and I shouted. Presently I heard one of my aunts calling reassuringly, 'What is it wee son?' At that moment the owlet flitted from the bed end and went out of sight behind the wardrobe. There was nothing to be seen when my aunt came hurrying into the room holding the oil lamp. I blinked and pointed to the fireplace.

'The wee owls were on the end of my bed!' I declared filled with excitement.

My aunt held the light higher and peered at me.

'Now son, just put your head on the pillow and get to sleep. There are no owls in the room! Owls are away at night about their own business. They don't come into wee boys' bedrooms.'

Reluctantly she made an inspection of the space behind the wardrobe and looked into the flue.

'There's nothing there at all,' she told me. 'You've been dreaming about the owls. We'll put the old wardrobe back tomorrow. It was likely the wind in the chimney that woke you up thinking the owls had got in.'

But I knew it wasn't, although I couldn't convince her that three owls had sat there on the end of my bed.

Years later, when I was sleeping upstairs, a similar thing happened. This time I was woken up by a perfectly feathered, very beautiful light mahogany-coloured barn owl that came and sat on the end of my bed. It stayed there blinking at me while I stared at it. On this occasion there was distinct evidence of its having perched for it had limed the floor and brought a lot of soot which it had scattered indiscriminately on everything in the room. All this was yet to come, however. My owlets were dismissed as a child's nightmare. To restore my nerves and make me forget the ordeal, I was given the rifle bullet pencil. I lost it in the years that followed but I needed no souvenir of that occasion to recall the time when the young owls paid me a visit.

The family's superstitions about birds and omens were so strong that it was an unwritten law that no one ever disturbed a bird living anywhere under our roof. I grew up quite indoctrinated with the idea that to harm them was something outrageous. When I was finally allowed to have a gun it was for the destruction of crows on the potato field, the discouragement of pigeons feeding on the corn, or the provision of a rabbit for the pot. If I ever shot anything in excess of our need I was made to eat it. 'Now,' my grandfather would say, 'if you point a gun, you must think before you shoot. If you shoot some harmless creature we don't have any reason to destroy, you eat it!'

To be truthful I was at first given to wanton killing and I had to eat more hare meat than I could sometimes stomach. I once shot a cuckoo, thinking it was a sparrowhawk, and was allowed to bury it in the kitchen garden before Grandfather returned from his morning trip to the creamery. Everyone urged me to get off to the wood with a piece in my pocket unless I wanted to eat that old cuckoo. There was, however, a symbol of wanton killing in the dining room, in the form of a stuffed owl. It was there before I came on the scene, at first in a handsome glass dome, borrowed from a clock that had finally stopped telling the time, and latterly after the glass had broken, exposed to the peat reek and the moth. It wasn't a barn owl, or one of the tawnies from the fir planting up where the burn had its source, draining the moor, but a long-eared owl from what we called the wholert moss. Long-eared owls lived not so much on the moss as in the pines and spruce trees that fringed that place. There is nothing that seems quite so ferocious as the baleful expression a taxidermist always seems to give a long-eared owl when he sets it up. The stuffed owl's ear tufts, which are not ears at all but feather adornments, make a shy, retiring bird look fierce. This owl on the mantelpiece glared at us through a thousand Sunday suppers and the smoke of a thousand blow-backs induced by winter gales. It was still glaring, I imagine, when someone opened the lobby door and a counterblast of wind, a draught to make the oil lamps blink, took it right off the mantel and tumbled it into the fire. In less than a minute the long-eared owl was cremated amidst an acrid fume of burning feathers and whatever rubbish the taxidermist had used to stuff its long-dried skin.

Time passed and the barn owls remained with us. It would have been a different house without them, for they were part of it, like the ancient tea rose or the flowering currant that stood by the steps down to the road. People who came to visit us on those long summer evenings when the place basked in the glow of a sinking sun would notice the owls coming onto the chimney stack in the gloaming and tell us how wonderful it was to have them living with us. Once the whole family of owls could fly they spread out over the fields mousing and calling to one another. Grandfather was well on in years, and I was by then living in Middlesex, when disaster came. A farmhand who had been allowed to get a rabbit for the pot came down the steading one evening and, seeing the owl sailing over the farmhouse roof, promptly put up the gun and killed it. The owl fell, a shattered corpse. Its feathers drifted across the slates and onto the grass of the wee field behind the house. My aunts, who were on their way back from locking up their hens, rushed at the unfortunate farmhand and snatched the gun from him, heaping recriminations on his head and promising he would depart never to return the moment Grandfather heard of his crime. Grandfather had been dozing in the sitting room but had seen the owl fall from the eaves. He came hurrying through in his stockinged feet so full of rage he could hardly speak. The farmhand rushed up the ladder to the loft and grabbed his possessions before returning to the kitchen. As my aunts had promised, he was sent packing there and then. His wages were sent after him. The owls never rested in the chimney again. Perhaps there was something in what my grandmother had always said.

Grandfather was already dead, and I was married and living far from the pastures of my boyhood, when what my aunts firmly believed was the working of a curse finally took place. My young cousin who was working the farm, and was the mainstay of his mother and aunt, suffered a ruptured appendix and died a very painful death. The farm had to be sold up. My aunts went into retirement in a lodge on the estate and never ever went back to look at their old home again. For my part, being descended from a witch and generations of peasants, I can't laugh at superstition. I am quite ready to believe that shooting an owl brings retribution. I have been careful never to shoot one myself.

6 CALL OF THE WILD GOOSE

Away back in his blacksmithing days, when my father was a boy, my grandfather took to using an already ancient fowling piece, a percussion-cap gun which he loaded either with shot or an assortment of chopped up pieces of metal. He probably got his substitute material by the bucketful from the smithy and when he ran out of shot, took his life in his hands by pouring it down the muzzle of his gun and tamping it down with the ramrod. That gun met its end after I came to stay with my grandparents: it burst, chopping a piece off Grandfather's right thumb and nicking his cheek. I carried the broken stock of the old fowling piece for several years, aping the old man when he went to get a rabbit with a more up-to-date hammergun. Grandfather's wildfowling was a practical exercise. He never went to shoot for fun but once in a while to get a goose for the family, although they were no more enamoured of goose than rabbit, or to oblige farmer friends who would enjoy eating one, and have the bonus of the elimination of a bird, which, with the help of nine others, daily ate as much as a sheep. Geese in those far-off days were assailed by far fewer guns and came in to the potato fields or the stubbles, particularly in October, with less suspicion than they have today. To listen to my elders was to conjure up a vision of thousands of geese planing down to the farm pastures and, in a single night, if they rested there, paddling the ground to mud and leaving it without a blade of grass. The geese, newly-arrived from the north-west after crossing thousands of acres of sea, were, I was told, so ravenous that they put their heads down and tore out the grass for twenty-four hours. This was no doubt one of those tales old men liked to tell, but I don't doubt that the geese came in great numbers and were encountered in places that they have long since been taught to avoid by shooting pressure. When he came to farm Grandfather's hunting fire had diminished. He had never really been a great killer of wild things but didn't discourage anyone who came about the place from shooting game or fowl.

Geese arrived one memorable winter when I was a child, coming low beneath snow clouds, flying up the hollow, and across the steading so low, someone remarked, that you could have knocked them out of the air with a hayrake. I remember being called to the door to watch the snow-bewildered geese coming out of wind borne snowflakes, their wingbeats making them somehow reminiscent of humans seen swimming in a swell of the sea. It was almost Christmas. Although it was less of an occasion by far than New Year, it was a feast we observed when relatives came home from England on holiday. One of our visitors was down from Glasgow. He had a fancy to eat a goose and begged Grandfather to shoot one for him. The old man got the gun and unhurriedly loaded it with powder and shot. I was fascinated as I watched him using the ramrod and placing the percussion cap on the nipple. I was ordered to stand back, but, despite the hand on my shoulder, craned forward to watch Grandfather on the front steps, a yard or so from the door. The geese were flying like phantoms. The snow covered the old man's beard. He brushed it away with the back of his hand before he put up the long, octagonal-barrelled gun. I was amazed when the flying geese became instantly invisible. Smoke from the burning powder folded back in the wind and then there was the thud of a greylag hitting the ground just behind the house. Geese still came on. I suppose a dozen could have been brought down with as many shots, but one was all that was wanted. The bird, when it was recovered, was still warm. I had never seen one at close quarters. It looked remarkably like our own domestic geese, so like them in fact, that I could hardly believe that it wasn't one of them. I had never seen any of the farm geese fly more than a foot or two from the ground, however, and that only when they were playfully chased by a collie pup. There it was, a goose from the grey northern sky, a wilderness in which nothing survived in winter but seals and polar bears. My mind was full of pictures put there by Grandmother who of course had only second-hand accounts to draw upon. Wild geese were part of winter. They impinged upon a sometimes grim world in which we might become snow-bound and the cart tracks, even when there was no snow, as hard as iron. Every slope on the public road would be glazed with ice, and horses found it difficult to haul a cart up one or hold it back on the way downhill.

There were days in October that marked the onset of winter even more distinctly than the slow thawing out of yesterday's newly-turned furrows, those clear, unnaturally bright days when the first of the geese came south. There are no words to describe the magic of these occasions. Summer turns to autumn with no significant change beyond a congregation of finches or swallows on the wires. There is nothing very dramatic about the departure of swallows. Their absence is a negative, and their arrival isn't heralded by anything out of the ordinary. They arrive. They flit in and out of their time-honoured haunts, their nesting places. After a few days have passed we come to realise they are there. But the wild geese are another matter. They talk to one another, babble in the cloudless depth of space and fly at the same marathon pace. Theirs is a rhythmic, tireless flight with no abrupt change in direction, but a slow, steady veering from north to east with perhaps no change of height the human eye could detect, although they probably make a descent from the moment they sight land, the far-off bays, estuaries and lochs to which they are heading. The cry of the wild goose spreads across the country. Farm geese, alerted by it long before the keenest human ear has detected the call, lift their heads from their grazing, cock an eye heavenward and begin to make a cry of their own. They stand and wait. They move their wings as though shortly they will exercise them and make a trial run before take-off, as indeed wild geese on the sands or pastures do when they are about to depart for some new feeding ground or roosting place. At such a moment even the over-weight Emden goose would take off if he could. The whole domestic flock would rise, circle and ascend to meet their kind and go with them to the distant sands. There is no doubt of this, as anyone who has witnessed the effect of the arrival of the migrants will agree. Before the geese are seen in the far-up heavens their sound becomes audible to the human ear and then the excited babbling of both domesticated and wild geese increases. The echelons and the line astern flights of greylags and pinkfeet stand out against the heavens. Thousands of geese come across the sky. They may be talking to the farm geese on the ground, but they show no sign that they are even aware of their presence. They have a place to go to. They have perhaps hours more to fly and the need to feed immediately the long journey is ended. They pass over. The farm geese go on babbling. Finally, when the migration is past, they waddle about their earthbound business, delving for food in the debris of the potato riddlings or the grass of the flooded hollow.

This encounter is an unutterably sad thing to witness. I watched it as a child and as a youth and never failed to be moved and affected by it, so much so that I have come to think that often it wasn't only the instinct of the domestic bird that was involved, but some deep-rooted interest of my own, as though my ancestors had had their days or their years marked by the arrival of the geese and their cry reverberates in my sub-conscious. I must not pretend that I never put up a gun at a goose. I did, but to be perfectly truthful, I took no pleasure in bringing one down and did very little of it. My ancestors certainly looked at the geese and reached for a gun or some other device with which to get as many for the pot as they could. For me the geese heralded the coming of the dark days of winter, the lowering of leaden skies and a wind that often took my breath away and hacked my hands. My elders were always depressed to think that if the greylags dropped on the fields of our farming friends the sheep would be deprived of their bite. They wouldn't have begrudged them the few potatoes still to be found in the black earth where the haulms had been raked away and burned. They could pick what the rooks and the pigeons hadn't already gleaned from the stubble, a frugal picking to be sure, but they weren't wanted where there was still grass. If they came sweeping in one day in early November, innocently advertising their arrival in the manner of their kind, Willie or someone else would be sent hurrying across the field to fire a shot and put them back into the air again. There was little point in firing at them. Even although they were as yet unused to the rattle of shot on their pinions, they knew the outline of their enemy. They had that special vigilance feeding geese always display, three or four always having their heads up while the rest have theirs down. A single shot would put them up. They would rise in a trailing line, beat over the distant meadow and finally skirt a hillock to disappear, at length, over the skyline. On the low meadows by the river they were left in peace because no creature without webbed feet could very well graze such inundated pasture. There, in the course of a few days, they learned they were safe. They would come over high in the morning and slide down to settle. In mid afternoon, after much debate, they would rise and head away to the safety of the sands. Men working on the higher land would hear them arriving and look for the morning tea basket and in the afternoon consider how much longer they had to plough or how long to suffer the agony of carting frozen swedes. In a week or two the geese took over from the distant train that whistled at exactly the same hour every night and morning, while daylight itself, getting shorter, needed some better kind of marker if the rising or the setting sun was lost in a misty haze.

The wild goose was a novelty for visitors. It was always something of a nine days' wonder for the country boy growing up, the boy who saw the cuckoo and the corncrake, the black cock coming down into the cornfield and the deer, in due time, standing on the wintery field where he hadn't been a moment before. Youths with guns, and old, incurable fowlers stalked the geese and shot them. Sometimes, sad to relate, they wounded them without being able to bring them down. Sometimes the crippled goose lagged far behind the flight and beat his own lonely way to the sands and starved and died. One such goose, a cripple, came up from the shore and lost his way to the meadows; perhaps he had been shed by the flight. Someone, standing on a whin-grown hill, tried to bring him down but had only succeeded in winging him. The wounded greylag couldn't make height again and came finally over the hill beyond the kitchen window, flying heavily, until he barely cleared the march dike and was compelled to crash land in what had been the old rickyard. This was a place overgrown with ragwort and weeds where the snows rooted and the farm geese made their way to the overflow of the byre midden. I was on my way to the dairy when my aunts called me.

'A wild goose has come down!' they cried. 'Come and see!'

I turned and ran to where they were. The greylag had just managed to right itself. It made no effort to take off but stood still, perhaps twenty yards from the farm geese. They also stood and stared. I suppose they recognized the wild bird but the wild one was less sure of them. When the gander of the domestic flock came stiffly towards him the wild one turned and walked away. The farm goose ran. The wild one flapped its wings and, despite its disability, managed to get far enough from the gander to discourage him from following. In a little while when the rest of the geese, five or six of them, Emden and Toulouse, were down in the trough below the old elm trees at the bottom of the rickyard, the wild goose walked towards them and began feeding. The family watched from the kitchen window, delighted to think that the wild goose was with us. It was still on the field when our geese returned to the steading and there the following morning when daylight came. Someone who had forgotten the incident remarked that one of our geese must have stayed out all night, but the same day there was a near disaster. The man who tended sheep beyond the march dike sent his dog round to cut off a wayward tup, and the dog, almost bounding onto the injured wild goose, took after it and caught it by the wing. In less than a minute one of my aunts had rushed out with a walking stick. The dog held the goose but when she came up to it she persuaded the dog to release its capture and the dog went over the dike with its tail between its legs. The poor goose lay stretched out, almost dead from shock, but after a little while it recovered and scuttled away. It had become part of the family. From this time on it was watched over. A special trough was put far enough out in the field for the wild goose to be comfortable there and mash was put in the trough so that it could feed. At first the farm geese gobbled up the mash, but somehow the wild one discovered what it was about and began to feed from the trough. It also took the corn that was liberally scattered near the trough. Day by day it seemed to get stronger and even a little less wild. It never actually mingled with the farm geese but it stayed with them and was tolerated. We would point it out to visitors as 'our wild goose'. It began to take low flights across the field. Everyone thought it was getting its wing muscles back in use so that it could join the first flight that came over. Once or twice we thought it had decided to go and look for its own kind, when, making a wide circuit, it got higher than usual, but it always came back to the field. Grandfather said the wild would call it back. It wouldn't stay. One day when he spotted a young man perched on a hill not far from our boundary he went off and gave him a 'ragging' for trying to ambush the goose. The old man was something of a terror when he was angry. Few people stayed to argue with him, and after this the goose managed to make its training flights without being shot at. We were all relieved about that, but we weren't so sure that it would ever get back to the far north when the great migration took place in spring. The wild birds, flying many miles to and fro every day, were capable of flying for hours on end. The bird we had fostered might fall behind or come down in the first windstorm. But Grandfather was not at all pessimistic. He said wild geese weren't fed good mash and corn morning and afternoon. Sometimes they found very poor pickings. Often the stubbles and old potato fields were turned over, leaving them nothing. Our goose would be strong. It would get there.

The day of its departure was heralded by goose talk. There was a mild breeze. The land was thawing, softening. Buds on bushes on the verge of marshes were fattening. Catkins were beginning to break and peewits were frequenting the arable fields. That particular morning our own geese stood still for a long time, their heads held high, all of them sentinels, one might have thought. They listened to the call of the wild geese. The wild goose out there on the rickyard field had gobbled his corn, fed on his mash. All at once he launched himself, flew round in a circuit of the steading and made another, wider circuit of the fields. All of this must have been timed for when he climbed up and went over the hill a long line of geese came from the south-west and he was just on time to fall in behind.

'He has gone. He has gone!' my aunts shouted.

But it was a very sad moment. I stared in the direction of the departing flight and tears sprang in my eyes. It was no consolation to see a second wave of geese coming. As my grandmother had often told me as she crooned me to sleep, the grey goose has gone . . .

He didn't come back. I looked for him the following day and for days afterwards. How can anyone ever know the fate of a wild creature that ranges over hundreds of miles between one season and another?

'We'll never see that goose again,' my aunts said, 'but he's happy, away there, across the wild sea, with his own kind.'

I couldn't go on grieving. Spring was too wonderful with such a blaze of morning sunrise at times, such a sweet scent of the awakened land at evening, and the birds singing. I forgot the wild goose. No misery is forever.

It was in October of that year that one of my aunts, out gathering mushrooms from the rickyard field, saw the solitary goose flying round. A single goose at any time would have been something to talk about, but after the previous winter and the arrival of the injured bird, what else could this lone goose be but the one that had sought refuge with us? There was great excitement. The goose didn't land but flew round and round for about ten minutes. Then it departed, going up and over the hill and away towards the sands. It didn't appear next day. My grand-father said it was all 'fun and fancy to please old Nancy' an expression he used for any wild flight of fancy. A goose had somehow lost its way and gone round and round trying to find its bearings. There were thousands of them. Then the same thing happened in November. The solitary goose came round again, making circuits of the farm. Ah well, Grandfather said, it could just be that it remembered where food had once been plentiful. My aunts rushed out and put mash in the trough and scattered enough corn for a flock. The visitor came again a third and a fourth time, but it never landed and that was the very last we ever saw of it.

7 TURKEY TROUBLES

If the man who came out of prison inspired to invent the hen battery had even begun to serve his sentence in those long ago days when nearly all farming in Britain could be called a peasant enterprise, no one in our family would have considered, even for a minute, keeping birds or other live stock in close confinement. The peasant system left ploughing and sowing to the male members of the family with help from other men waged by the 'term' or the year. The women concerned themselves with the dairy and the fowls. A man 'mucked out' the piggery which was kept spotlessly clean, but the pigs ranged free and turned the turf of old pastures where no other animals grazed but geese. Along with their many other duties my aunts reared and looked after ducks. While my grandmother was alive she kept turkeys because she knew how to rear them. Turkey rearing, even with modern equipment and antibiotics, can be a hazardous business. Young turkeys have to be most carefully looked after or they will go down like flies with chills or infection picked up before they have a cultivated resistance to disease. In much the same way as she managed the dairy, Grandmother had an authority when she set about producing an annual brood of turkeys. There was money in it, but shillings rather than pounds when a dozen fresh eggs would fetch only pence, and a pound of butter not much more.

I have two early recollections of the turkey rearing. A much pampered and indulged child, I would be sat in at the breakfast table and brought up to the right level with a cushion on the chair. A feeder would be tied round my neck and I would be left to tackle a breakfast egg with neat little fingers of buttered bread to dip in the yolk. In the beginning my egg was topped for me, but I had no patience when I thought I had grasped the principle of a thing, and would brush aside the hand that tried to feed me, or top my eggs! One morning I was settled in to have my breakfast when they came from behind with an enormous egg-cup. I think it would have taken a goose egg, but on this occasion what it held was a beautiful cream-coloured turkey egg. It was such a lovely sight that I didn't want to start on it, but there it was, and I was urged not to let my breakfast get cold. At length I hacked through the top and began to delve inside with the spoon and to mop up the rich yolk with those butter-finger sections of white bread. The egg was one Grandmother had superfluous to her needs. It was delicious and I somehow managed to eat it all. It was the first turkey egg I had ever seen. If I had never seen a turkey egg, I had, however, seen the old turkey cock, an enormous bird who seemed to move on castors like a piece of furniture, and would put his wings down and drive even the dogs out of his territory. He terrified me. As soon as I tried to cross to the stable or go up to the cart shed, he would be there, threatening me, driving me back. He, like the smithy raven, recognized that a boy's legs were a particularly vulnerable part of his body, and he always went for mine, bringing tears to my eyes when he hit me. I would run for home and the enfolding comfort of my aunts who consoled me with sweet biscuits from a special tin, or sometimes a hot scone from the girdle. Grandfather was less sympathetic. I should turn round and stand up to the old 'bubbly', he said. There was nothing else for it. If I turned on him he would run. No matter how the turkey cock coloured up, no matter how formidable were his rushes, he was a coward. If I rushed him when he came at me, I would find that he would be off like a sheep-worrying dog. One morning I would gather my courage and face him, and he would never chase me again! Did I not see that? The cock of the walk only picked on those who ran. I didn't need to arm myself with a stick, or kick him the way the byre boy kicked out at the old bull when he seemed to threaten me. All I needed to do was stop and take two or three steps towards my tormentor and he would turn and run. I would find this with men as well as turkey cocks. A man who was too timid to stand his ground was put upon. A man who faced his tormentors could make them run. The little lecture didn't give me as much as an ounce of confidence. That monster bird with a kind of hairy tassle dangling from his breast bone would arch his neck, gobble his irritation and come like a train. There seemed to be a day coming when I would stand and give battle. Occasionally my exposed legs (my socks had a habit of going down round my ankles no matter how often I pulled them up) were lacerated. The pugnacious bird would hit me with his beak, strike me with his feet, and beat me with his wings, all in one terrifying onslaught. I was in terror of being knocked down and pecked to death and only went up through the steading when the tyrant was nowhere to be seen.

'Take a bit of stick with you,' my aunts advised. 'Slash at the old devil, knock him over!'

I knew it would never happen. One day when I thought I had the place to myself I went up through the steading. There wasn't a sign of the old bubbly anywhere. Cats were lying in the shelter of the limestone buildings. Red and blue pigeons sunned themselves on the ridge. I was always carried away by the sight of such things. The twittering of a bird, the drone of a bumble bee were music in a child's ears. I was half-way to the shed where he had been lurking on his own. I ran, and he came scuttling after me, the stiff pinions of both wings scraping on the ground. My heart thudded. I would have screamed, but no sound came; then, just as he was about to overtake me, my hand somehow grasped a short length of rope hanging over the rim of a potato barrel and I turned in sheer desperation and lashed at him. To my astonishment the great fat monster fell off his feet, flapped, made noises and scrambled to escape the lash. A wild, vengeful rage possessed me. I whirled the rope and rushed after him. He diminished in size, diminished visibly for he no longer fluffed himself up in that characteristically threatening posture. He raced away, a slim bird with a flaccid, dangling comb. I couldn't catch up with him, but I had managed to give him two whacks and rout him. I had never been so pleased with myself. I went back to the farmhouse, showed them my piece of rope, and told them how I had put old bubbly to flight. Dear me, how they praised me. I was a brave wee man. I was cock of the walk. They always knew I would put that wicked old bubbly in his place. Full of bravado, I marched off out again and up through the steading. I had somehow frightened away the basking cats. The homing pigeons had gone from the ridge, although swallows darted about, catching flies. For a minute or two I half-expected the turkey cock to come at me again and I wondered if I could terrify him a second time. I looked for him. He was nowhere to be seen. My confidence growing, I went to find him. He was down by the side of the midden and saw me coming and made desperate efforts to get through the mud and avoid being lashed. I held my piece of rope less tightly in my hand. I saw him as nothing more than an ordinary turkey. He had lorded it over me and persecuted me, the way he somehow managed to frighten the dogs, but now even the dogs were there, standing behind me. I didn't set them on him. He was no longer a terror. When I crossed the court after that he kept well clear of me. If he happened to be 'inflated' when I arrived he quickly reduced himself to normal proportions and was careful to head away from me, even when I didn't have my short length of rope. The dogs who were my companions gained courage and, instead of turning tail when they met the old bubbly, would rush him, cut him off and threaten him until he was deflated and ran, ignominiously for shelter.

'So you mastered him?' Grandfather said when he came in for his tea in mid-afternoon that day. 'Did I not tell you what you had to do? You are growing up, my boy!'

Looking back I know well that I grew up that day. Not long after this the old man demonstrated his own belief that a man must stand his ground. The old Galloway bull was suddenly taken with a kind of madness that comes upon old bulls when their virility is diminishing. Old Johnny began to bellow and tear the ground with his foot. The sound could be heard for miles. He had gone 'bad', they said and, remembering poor Uncle James, who had ignored a similar state of affairs, and gone out to look at his herd one morning only to be battered into the ground and brutally killed, it was important to house the old Galloway and send for the butcher. There would be another tragedy if the bull wasn't put down. Grandfather and one of his men went out and brought the bull down from the hill with the help of the dogs. The straw house was chosen as a prison because it had no windows and was a stone building with a stout door. Old Johnny would stand in darkness until the butcher came. Alas, while he was being herded towards the narrow door, old Johnny put his head down and made a rush towards Grandfather and he had nothing with which to defend himself but his walking stick. There, before the womenfolk and myself, none of us with anything to hand with which to turn a red-eyed, snorting bull, Grandfather stood his ground. He was 'lame of a leg' and had been so since boyhood. He couldn't run. He used the stick like a sword and actually advanced. The bull could hardly see. It slavered and bellowed. It must have weighed more than a ton. If it had no horns it had that heavy bone on its skull that bulls of this breed have, making them into a battering ram. Somehow the message reached the small brain in the old bull's shaggy head. He stopped pawing the ground and retreated, step by step, until he was prodded towards the door. Finally he went in at a half gallop, his soiled tail swinging as the door was slammed shut. My aunts rushed to their father. The old man blinked and said, 'God damn it, he's only an old bull and he knew I wasn't feared of him.' Having delivered himself of this assertion he went off to bring the butcher. The bull in due course provided as much brisket and rump steak for as long as meat would keep in those days. The incident with the bull under-lined the lesson I learned from the turkey cock. What I really dis-covered was that a time comes when every man must stand by himself both physically and mentally.

Grandmother's turkey-rearing went on for years. When she was no longer there my aunts took over. As in all domestic things, they had been well schooled. When Grandmother died they made the same wonderful blackberry wine, the same mushroom ketchup, the same shortbread. In the dairy they made butter the way she had made it. It wasn't surprising that when it came to it they were equally successful with turkeys. I remember one winter, however, when all their labour proved in vain. The birds had been fed their special mixture, cosseted and tended with loving care, week after week and month after month, until they were almost ready for market. One grim morning in Decem-ber when they went to open the henhouse door they were alarmed by the unusual silence. The henhouse hadn't a bird in it! Hardly a feather was to be seen. The entire flock of turkeys had been bagged up and spirited away in the small hours, and not a dog had barked! The policeman was summoned and walked round looking for footprints in the mud, or feathers which might have adhered to the sacks the thieves had carried away. The sacks had come from our own barn. Enquiries were made far and wide. All that was discovered was that we were not alone. Two other farmers had been robbed at the same time. It seemed obvious that such a large haul of birds had to be taken far away before they could be offered for sale. It seemed obvious too, that the thieves were local. They knew the buildings. They probably knew the dogs. Grandfather raged and stormed and then sat down and worked out who the thieves were likely to be, but however shrewd his guess might have been, and however many times the police went to question the same set of desperate characters, no result came of it at all.

The Bible says there is a time for all things, a time to sow and a time to reap, and there was, of course, no chance of the turkey thieves being caught in the act until there were turkeys reared and grown big enough for the market. The whole business of turkey breeding may prove a loss if the birds are brought on before market time, or if they aren't at the best possible weight when they have to go. The experts today may have it all worked out down to the last milligramme and the unit of heat, but even in those bad old days those farmers' wives knew a thing or two about the economics of turkey rearing. My aunts contrived to have their young turkeys coming along at exactly the right time. They were careful in their feeding. They knew all too well about draught and damp. They never counted their birds until they were well-grown. From this experience they knew when they would set about the annual chore of getting the birds ready for market, plucking and trussing them as they always had done. The turkey thieves knew, of course, that they had to make their raid before this happened or the birds that would go to market would have been put under lock and key after being prepared for the oven. Grandfather knew when to expect the raid. The thieves had come once and got away with perhaps thirty plump birds and made a lot of money. He would be ready for them the following year and have the place booby-trapped with wire and cans. The dogs could fraternise if they liked.

'I am not going to see the labour of a whole summer stolen!' the old man swore. 'This time I will sit up for them with the gun!'

Such an exercise my aunts felt was fraught with danger. What if Grandfather shot and killed one of the intruders? There was no telling what might happen. The old man was quite determined. He looked at the young turkeys and the calendar and decided when his vigil would begin. He had told no one outside the family that he was going to sit up with the gun. My aunts thought at first that they would somehow spirit the cartridges away, but when he discovered these were not in their usual place he demanded that they be brought to him. Reluctantly they brought the box back and put it on the shelf of the cupboard.

'Will you really shoot them, Grandfather?' I asked. To tell the truth I was rather excited by it all. I had a vision of a thief being bowled over like a hare as he ran through the court with a sack of turkeys on his back.

'I will that!' Grandfather promised.

My aunts shook their heads. He never would, they said, even although he swore that by God he would. Before he kept his first vigil he went off out to the dairy with a lump of rock salt which he pounded with a hammer. I watched, fascinated as he sorted the broken salt and removed the lead shot from half a dozen cartridges. My aunts were unaware of this reloading for he did it all down in the sitting room, pouring the lead into a pouch, filling the cartridges one by one and replacing the wads which he afterwards sealed with beeswax.

'Now,' he told me confidentially, 'if I hit one of them with the hard salt it will cut them, but it won't do them much harm! They won't go running to say how they got shot because they daren't do that, but if they do who will find shot under their skin anyway?'

Years afterwards I wondered if the rocksalt might have put out the man's eye and shuddered to think of the risk the old man took, but when he pocketed his ammunition I thought it was a very cunning thing he was doing. The thieves would get the fright of their lives. That night, instead of going to bed, Grandfather went out and sat in the entrance to the building adjoining the turkey shed, making himself comfortable and warm among straw and bags of chaff. He wasn't going to smoke he told me, in case the smell of his tobacco betrayed him. He was just going to wait there until they came and he would let them go into the shed. They would have their medicine when they came out. I tried to stay awake that night but couldn't. I awoke in the morning having forgotten Grandfather had gone and watched. For once he wasn't there to take the milk to the creamery. He was upstairs in bed, my aunts told me. The turkeys were alright. No shot had been fired and they were thankful for that. Maybe if he had had a night or two of nothing happening Grandfather would change his mind or move the flock into the strawhouse. Grandfather wasn't to be persuaded, however. He had no intention of moving the birds. He wanted revenge for last year and he was prepared to suffer to punish the thieves. Again he sat up without results, but the passing of three days convinced him the thieves would come now. He took a small bottle of whisky with him because the nights were getting colder and colder. At last it happened. The moon was up. The thieves could see their way about. They came as before and talked to the dogs. They didn't look into the darkness of the stonehouse beside the turkey shed, but went for the sacks and came back to harvest their reward. Grandfather fired on them as they came out. The yells, the howls of agony as well as the second and third blasts of the gun as the old man reloaded and fired again, awakened everyone.

'God help us,' one of my aunts wailed, rushing down to struggle into a coat, 'he hasn't killed somebody has he?'

I can remember the cold floor under my bare feet and the wind blowing the door back. Grandfather came across the court, his face enshadowed because his back was toward the moon.

'Let the poor birds get back in the shed,' he said, 'and get yourselves back to your beds, they won't come here again.'

Grandfather saw his suspects at the market a few days later and, so I was told, turned aside and asked, 'Now, how did you boys get cut about the head like that? What were you up to? Were you poaching or something?' His victims cursed him and told him to mind his business. He said he was very good at doing that as anybody who came about his farm could tell them.

8 THE SURFEIT OF GUINEAS

In my childhood country women who worked hard at all the domestic chores still somehow found time to do more than simply feed hens and put saucers of milk for cats. In due season they would contrive to meet one another and arrange for an exchange of a setting of eggs or the supply of a much needed broody hen. It was this keen interest in breeding fowl that brought us a surfeit of guineas which ended so tragically. There wasn't a guinea fowl about the place until my Aunt Ellen brought them. Ellen was the more out-going of my father's two sisters and her need for social contact was strong. She would hie herself off to whist drives and suppers whenever the occasion presented itself. She travelled miles, sometimes on her bicycle and sometimes across country on foot, to visit neighbours. When she went on foot she would carry her best shoes in a brown paper parcel so that they weren't muddied by the journey across rough ground. When she reached the hard road she would change out of her old shoes, wrap them in the same piece of brown paper and stow them somewhere behind a drystone wall, in a gorse bush, or even down a rabbit hole where she could recover them when she returned. On this particular occasion she came back while it was still light. It was midsummer and daylight lingered on towards midnight. The old shoes had been stowed in a bracken clump and, her mind full of the conversation she had enjoyed and the titbits of gossip imparted to her, Ellen couldn't recall exactly where she had hidden her old shoes. It was imperative that they be found and exchanged for her best ones for there were a number of 'gutters' to be forded on the way home. In the process of seeking that which was lost my aunt flushed a guinea fowl out of a clump of round rushes and immediately went to investigate. Guinea fowl are more prone to making wild nests than bantams. Birds of African origin, they love the wilderness and insist upon nesting in a private place. This particular bird came from a nearby farm. It had ventured well out of sight of the steading and laid its eggs on a nest in a secluded hollow close to the road along which my aunt travelled. The clutch of pointed, buff-coloured eggs was a delight to my aunt. She gathered it, taking her hat off and using it as a basket. Having at last found her hidden away shoes she went to the farm to tell the farmer's wife of her discovery. The lady concerned had no need of eggs. She had too many guinea fowl and too many eggs. Bells should have rung in my aunt's head at that but she was full of gratitude for the gift and took herself home carefully carrying her prize. Our neighbour's wife warned her as she departed not to let the thing get out of hand. A body could have more guineas than he needed! Her husband abominated the creatures and said they sat in the trees like vultures and ate corn before the hens could get to it. But aunt went off in a dream of beautiful fowl that picked their way about the court and looked as lovely as a laird's peacocks.

There was no need to go in search of a broody hen. Two or three were available to sit on the guinea hen's clutch. On the following morning the project was launched and a White Wyandote settled on the guinea fowl eggs. The brooding coop was a barrel set on its side and lodged in position with a couple of stones. No matter what people said about the difficulty of raising guinea chicks, they would have success! My aunts were experts in this kind of husbandry. They cossetted the White Wyandote and saw that she wasn't disturbed and in due course the hen brought off her large hatch of youngsters, handsome, sturdy, grey-legged chicks that crowded round their enormous mother. I remember wondering what a hen hatching an unusual brood makes of it when the chicks are so unlike her own kind. The White Wyandote seemed totally unaware that these were not the ordinary domestic fowl but an entirely different breed brought to Britain maybe by the Romans when they brought the bantam and the Phoenician fowl. The keeper called and told my aunts he wouldn't have guinea within a mile of his place. They drove away pheasants. They would murder cockerels. But my aunts were not in the least discouraged. They loved novelty whether it was a black sheep or a Manx cat. The White Wyandote was a jealous mother and drove off every creature that came within yards of her brood, teaching more than one of the slinking farm cats a lesson when they attempted to get themselves a dinner. The brood thrived. There were at least fourteen youngsters and they ran merrily after their scratching parent, pouring over mounds, fluttering onto walls in order to follow her. There were no losses. The chicks grew and Grandfather noticed them.

'God's sake lassies,' he said, 'What do you want with birds like that? They grow to look like vultures and they do a lot of damage they tell me.'

The 'lassies' denied that the guinea fowl was like a vulture and asked who knew anything about vultures anyway? Old Jack who had been in Africa on foreign service, chipped in with his two-pennyworth and said he had seen vultures picking the bones of dead men. They told him that when the guinea fowl began picking his bones he would be long dead! But they kept quiet about the damage a guinea fowl might do. Already our neighbour was having to put wire netting on his ricks for guinea fowl were busy tearing away the thatch.

One day at some farmers' dinner or other the old man had a plate of guinea fowl meat. He came home and told his daughters they might continue keeping their birds so long as they didn't cost too much. Their flesh was as good as pheasant or partridge, and he was very fond of partridge. I doubt whether my aunts could have been persuaded to give up their fowl by this time. They had become attached to them and often sighed and said how delighted my grandmother would have been to see them about the steading.

Grandmother would indeed have been delighted to see the guinea fowl about the place because she loved animals, but Grandfather was an essentially practical man and, although he didn't begrudge the corn for that first brood of ridge-roosting fowl which he saw more and more to be like vultures, he became anxious about the way they multiplied. This was because the guineas had all the food they could eat, being able to sail over the drystone walls, get down into the sheds and places where they could rob the trough of rich protein pigmash, calves' food, the very grain the ploughman laddled into the stable troughs for his team if he forgot to close the stable door. Grandfather had one serious weakness apart from a built-in impatience with anything that got in his way. He had an ungovernable temper. He raged and called on God to damn things to hell and in his worst fits would dash his hat on the ground and stamp one foot. I always found these self-indulgent fits of passion very comical and if he saw me smiling it only made things worse. He was never violent in his reaction. His gravest threat was to 'bumph' my backside with the folded newspaper. The guinea fowl nuisance worried my aunts. If Grandfather wasn't allowed to cool down he would take drastic action and perhaps have the necks of the whole flock wrung. For days Grandfather uttered this threat, generally at the meal table, and almost always when the guineas were setting up a chorus of 'Come back! Come back!', a call that reminded me of the grouse on the moor. The old man would drop his spoon in his soup plate, half push back his chair and swear, 'I declare to my God I'll make an end of them!' Most of us would look down at our plates and get on with the business of taking soup or whatever we were eating, but my Aunt Mary, a diminutive, witch-like woman, could never control her tongue. Her own temper was very like the old man's and she would tell him, 'You'll do no such thing, Father! You'll let them alone! You declare anything you like to God, but you're not going to harm the poor birds!' Grandfather didn't like anyone coming between him and his message to God but, being lame and not very fast on his feet, he had no hope of catching even one of the guinea fowls. He would turn to one of his men and say, 'When you have your dinner done, Willie, you will get out there and wring the necks of every one of those pests. God's curse on them!' Such talk only provoked my God-fearing aunt more and she would accuse the old man of blasphemy and they would have an argument about the nature of blasphemy and whether he was cursing something or praying God to do it for him. Growling like an old dog, Grandfather would have more important things to think about than that plague of grey vultures that looked down from the roof tops and the branches of the old elms at the bottom of the disused stackyard.

'Try not to get your Grandfather going about the guinea fowl,' my aunt would tell me. 'One of these days he'll have them all killed if you let him see you think its funny!'

It gradually dawned on me that Grandfather was content to complain and call on God without doing anything about the nuisance. The Guinea fowl went forth and multiplied. They nested in the docks, in the nettles, in the briars and behind any bit of sheet iron left lying against a wall. They brooded their eggs where we forgot to look for them or where we had just gathered a clutch and thought they wouldn't lay another, and soon more and more guinea chicks were discovered filing from out of the growing corn and the ragwort, the hardheads and the thorns. They even went up and nested in the beehive enclosure as a pair of partridges did. We were said to be 'hoatching' with them, which means over-run by them, infested as a beggar might be infested with lice or a dog with fleas. Friends who came stared in amazement and fell silent when my aunts gave them warning looks or put a finger to their lips for the sake of peace and quiet. Oddly enough Grandfather himself ceased to mention the plague. It was so evident to everyone that he needed no one to remind him. He was then at his most dangerous and my aunts, who had themselves to admit that the whole thing had become a bit of a nightmare, said that he would blow up on one of these days and the guinea fowl would be destroyed. I remember our relative, the horse-dealer, coming to talk about a mare the old man was planning to enter for the next show, and Grandfather breaking off the conversation to say to no one in particular, 'We have guinea fowls here the way other folk have rats and the time is coming when the plague must pass or I'll have to do something!' Our relative cleared his throat to say something in reply but said nothing, knowing how volatile the old man's temper was. Another old friend, Frank McWilliam, was less tactful. 'John', he said, 'I would have thought you had more sense than let them be about your place. God's sac' hand, everybody knows the damage they do!' But for once Grandfather held his temper in check. 'There is a time for everything,' he said. He was fond of quoting scripture and loved Isaiah! When I was brain-washed with scripture, a little later on, I was surprised that Isaiah had said nothing about a time to wring the necks of pestilential guinea fowl, but Grandfather had a more violent end planned for them, though he revealed his plans to none of us.

A time to sow and a time to reap . . . the plague was still with us after harvest and all through the following winter. The ricks were threshed out or taken apart so that sheaves could be carted to the high barn and put through the built-in walk mill.* Every rick had a certain number of wet and wasted sheaves because the rain had penetrated where the thatch had been torn away by the guinea fowl. There were far too many ricks to be protected for them to be netted effectively. No one said much about the wasted corn. Mounds of wet sheaves told their own story. The guinea fowl screeched from the ridge and flew down to glean corn dropped below the high barn door as the dry sheaves were forked from the cart. Grandfather had nothing to say to his daughters about the loss. They said nothing because they were guilt-ridden. There must by this time have been between thirty and fifty well-grown, noisy birds roosting in the trees and high places. They liked the ridge on warm dry nights but they knew when the weather was going to change and found roosts in the lea when a gale was threatening. They took over the convenient perches in the cart shed. They moved the rightful occupants of these perches out of the sheds to huddle miserably elsewhere. They were tyrannical towards every other fowl. The ducks evaded them. Only the geese held their ground and waddled disdainfully past them. It took the collie to put them to flight and when he sent them flapping frantically onto the roof they scolded and complained and kept up their clamour for an hour or so afterwards. It didn't help when, taking his milk to the creamery in the morning, Grandfather was told by someone that his screeching fowl could be heard two or three miles away. When was he going to take them to market? Would they fetch the kind of price he had been hoping for? The joke of course was that everyone knew he had never intended to have the grey vultures and they were a scourge upon him.

My Great Aunt Ellen came and said her piece about the plague. She was never tactful and in fact she loved to irritate her brother-in-law.

'You would think he was a laird,' she said, 'keeping all those fowl! What can he be thinking? How many eggs would they lay in a year

* a horse-powered gear for threshing corn.

anyway? Two dozen if that! And do you ever eat them? I don't know what my sister would say to such extravagance!'

These remarks were to her nieces, my aunts, but they were intended to be overheard. Great Aunt Ellen loved to rub salt in Grandfather's wounds and when she departed she couldn't resist telling him to his face that his weaknesses were multiplying in his old age. It was a shame that all her dear sister had done to make the place pay was being brought to nothing by her husband's self-indulgence. This parting shot sealed the fate of the guinea fowl. The old man brooded and went off to town and came back with several boxes of cheap cartridges. He had made up his mind at last. It just happened that there was a mid-week preaching meeting down at the schoolhouse and both my aunts had arranged to attend. They were deeply religious, but there was also the never mentioned bonus of social contact, the conversations with neighbours on their way to and from the meeting and the exchange of titbits of gossip that were as important as The Word itself.

The old man made sure they were off to the meeting before he got the gun from the side of the grandfather clock and brought out his ammunition. He had no intention of doing the job himself. Willie, who had once been told to wring the necks of those uncatchable fowl, was to have an evening's shooting such as he had never had in his life before. He would rid every ridge, every tree, every perch, of the pests and go on shooting until he had done so!

Willie's prowess as a marskman wasn't terribly important. The wretched guinea fowl didn't know what it was about at first and then it was the noise of the gun that troubled them more than the casualties Willie's gun inflicted upon them. Shot tore lichen from the slates and splattered against the stonework of gables and fowl fell or came sliding down the slates to crash into the steading. Feathers were lost and the beleaguered birds flew from one place to another, even onto the old sow stack of straw in the rickyard. Grandfather stood at the kitchen door and refrained from giving advice or orders. Willie came back at intervals for another handful of cheap, multi-coloured cartridges with which he killed the birds. At length only two or three remained and they dodged to and fro, eluding Willie as best they could while he crept under the shelter of eaves or behind walls to come up with them. It was well past his supper time, when, wading into the midden to get within range of the last surviving fowl, he finally took careful aim and brought that one down. It interred itself by dropping into the morass below the midden and Willie, stepping carefully, extricated himself from the mire and threw away the last empty cartridge case. He took his meal and gathered the dead birds and buried them in the midden before my aunts returned from their outing. It was dusk by the time they did and there was no other sound to be heard but the faint, squeaky conversations of hunting owls and the far-away purring of a nightjar hawking moths across the moss.

My aunts made their usual 'wee cup of tea' before they prepared for bed. Neither asked what the gunfire had been about. Aunt Mary gave her father hard looks. Her sister, Ellen, behaved as though nothing had happened. Although they hadn't been there to witness the fearful slaughter both knew exactly what had been done. In the morning when the old man came in for his breakfast, having prepared for the creamery run, Aunt Mary looked him in the eye and asked him how much he expected to get for the fowl, supposing Gunning, the game dealer, would buy them.

Grandfather put his pipe in his waistcoat pocket, tapped his egg and cut his fingers of bread before he spoke.

'There was nothing but loss in it from the very beginning,' he said. 'Lost time, lost corn, ruined stacks! I had Willie bury them in the midden. I don't want to hear another word from either of you about it because it was your fault they came here in the first place!'

For once my aunt held her tongue. There was no denying that they had brought it all on their own heads. Everyone for miles around knew what the shooting had been about. It was old John getting rid of the plague he had put up with for so long. The wonder was that he had let it happen, but down underneath he was a soft man, a bit of a sentimentalist when it came down to it, and no farmer can ever afford to be a sentimentalist about animals or fowl.

9 MALLARD ON THE MOSS

The word mallard was never used to describe the commonest species of wild duck when I was a child. We didn't see wigeon very often. The 'wee teal' was a kind of toy duck that would paddle frantically downstream if anyone walked along the bank of the burn before it rose to skim away. The wild bird, mallard duck or drake, was almost a duplicate of the farmyard duck and there was no better name for it. We saw them dropping down to the corn on a misty evening. They rose with a rasping cry from the rushes of the bog. Their flesh was stronger and darker than that of the homebred species and no one bothered to shoot them so long as there were partridges and pheasants to be got. Such fowl fascinated me from an early age, beginning with the water hens that nested on the burn. Waterhens had been there since time immemorial despite the fact that someone always milked the nest of the first lot of eggs to provide a delicacy for breakfast. The egg is as tasty as that of a plover and often I was taken to stand by while someone waded into the burn to get an egg. The waterhen always hid in overhanging thorns or some secret place under the bank to emerge when intruders had departed. It was this kind of thing that made me an inveterate birdnester from the age of five. There wasn't a lot of harm in any of it bearing in mind the abundance of game and birdlife at that time. The Estate keeper kept down hawks, stoats and weasels. There wasn't a fox within thirty miles. We still had the corncrake in the hayfield. Nightjars purred from their perching places on the lichened march wall where our arable field flanked the wilderness of the wee moss. The moss wasn't really a moor. It was the site of a wood, a kind of guttery marsh dotted with peat mounds and gorse clumps. Occasionally a shaggy bullock floundered and struggled through the water-logged peat to come to the wall or the stretch of rusty, wire fence that divided a flooded peat drain. There had been a time when peat had been cut and carted from that particular corner. The excavation had left a natural pond of whisky-coloured water from which alder and bog myrtle grew to scent the summer air. I loved the place but I was constantly warned to keep away from it. A horse had drowned there once, they said, the ground giving way under its weight and the peaty water flowing round it until it foundered and disappeared into a kind of black porridge. I couldn't resist going up to the wee moss to look for the nest of a whaup or some other moor bird. I loved to breathe that special air and stand and listen to a yellowhammer singing its song over and over again, that heart-breaking, plaintive refrain about a little bit of bread and no cheese.

On that very first occasion I had gone up in the middle of the morning. It was May. The flourish-may blossom was just breaking on the green thorn tree. Little islands of gorse on marshy land that ended at a bank below a drystone wall were bright with butter-yellow blossom. My grandmother made wine from the whins some years when their colour was particularly strong. I had prospected one of the ditches on the way up, looking for nests on its bank, and watched the whinchats flitting over the moss. It was past the time for the peewit or the whaup to lay. I had found the nests of partridges on the banks of all the likely fields and a hen pheasant sitting on a clutch of eggs laid in the middle of a coil of old fence wire. The mallard would have gone back just before it disappeared behind a heather clump. I knew it wasn't a hare for a hare would have kept to the dry ground and I would have seen it again before it had gone many yards. Young as I was, I knew the wild duck was nesting close at hand, but I had no idea where to look. The nest could have been in the rushes close by the peat drain or on my side of the water in another heather clump. I looked everywhere but found nothing. The mallard, having travelled in that characteristically furtive way of a nesting duck, finally launched itself into the air making a slow circuit of the land on both sides of the boundary. I watched it and saw it look about. It saw me too and I knew it wouldn't land near its nest. After a while it planed down in the wilderness and disappeared out of sight. I knew it wasn't heading back to where I had put it up. After a while I took myself off to find a chaffinch's nest out on a bough I couldn't reach and then a brood of thrushes low in a bush. The farmhand who had instructed me in the art of bird-nesting said that the best way of discovering a nest was to go away and come back later, watching more carefully the second time. A peewit, for instance might rise in the same place every time but before it took flight it generally travelled on the ground without being noticed. A wild 'juke' was wily and a master at making itself invisible. I came back again the following day. The mallard, hearing my footfalls on the harder arable ground before I got to the marsh, eluded me again. All I saw was its slow circuit when it took to the air. A third and then a fouth approach convinced me it nested somewhere near the beginning of the fence and not far from the drystone wall. The heather wouldn't bloom for nearly two months. It's stalks were brown and a perfect blend with the plumage of a duck and I could have stared at it without seeing it. I looked for something else, of course, for a duck plucked its own down to cover its eggs and I hoped that the smallest bit of down, caught up when the duck moved, might lie close to the invisible nest. There was no such marker and I had to come again before I found what I was looking for.

The whole thing is indelibly etched in my mind because, I suppose, there was nothing wilder than a wild duck except the geese that only came down in winter and never stayed to nest. The wild duck was much more dramatic in its flight than a cock pheasant that sprang up from the pasture, crowed and went down in the next field. It was a bird that came out of the mist unexpectedly, passed over in company with two or three others, and belonged not just to a field or a particular farm, but the whole landscape. Even as a child I knew it, and imagined it flying half-way round the world. I could imagine the duck going beyond the horizon like the plume of smoke from the London-bound train and here it was nesting on the wee moss. Other children might have fairy fantasies, but mine were nature dreams. I ran with the galloping hare. I looked down on the world of water-logged meadows and winding rivers, flying with the duck. Now I was close to it, closer than I had ever been, and of course, I had to find the nest. I did so at last, for there was a single downy feather on the black peat and I saw where the bird had laid in a little depression on the bank almost entirely screened by heather stalks cascading from above. Where the duck was at that moment I don't know. It probably stood still out there among the water-filled peat holes and listened for some sound of pursuit. I gazed in wonder at the mass of down covering the eggs but didn't put my hand into it. I had been told many times that a bird has the sharpest eye for anything not as it had left it, and would forsake it if its eggs were moved. I had a secret and although I was bursting to tell someone, I managed to keep it to myself. Every day I went stealthily up to the waterhole and sat on the bank to watch, and the duck, already incubating, stayed on the nest. I could see the brown feathers of her back. She didn't move. Once, when I had begun to think she had died or had been killed where she sat by a marauding stoat, she glided off her eggs quite unexpectedly and went round the pool to feed. I don't know how many days passed in this way but before the brood hatched my daily visits to the place were noticed by my elders.

'What takes you up the ditch every day?' one of my aunts asked me. 'You're not bothering that pheasant sitting in the wire, are you?'

The pheasant had hatched her brood days before and, like all ground-nesting birds, had moved her chicks as soon as they could run. The nest contained nothing but olive-coloured shells. I didn't say anything about the duck for they would have prevented me going up to where the horse had drowned. My 'innocence' deceived no one. They knew there was something, and a day or two later while I was sat there half-drugged by the scent of gorse, may blossom and bog myrtle, I was startled by my aunt's hand on my shoulder. She had come to see for herself what drew me like a magnet to that corner.

The duck slipped away this time, disturbed by the sound of our whispered conversation, but it stood on the bank twenty yards from the nest and stayed there. I was led away and gently lectured all the way back to the farm. I might drown if I went nearer that bank, I was told. The nest was like the side of the midden below the byre. After rain it heaved and always the bank slipped farther into the mire. The alder that stood all by itself in the water had once been on a bank. I must never go there again! I had been forbidden to go to certain burns where trout could be fished for with a worm because the best places were deep. After rain, when the trout were feeding, many of the burns were as dangerous as the flooded river but I didn't always do as I was told. I had a habit of allowing myself to be carried away by a dream. More than once I toppled into the water and got all my clothes wet so that I had to be stripped and put in a tub when I got home. The tubbing involved a lot of water-boiling and water-carrying, a hard scrubbing with carbolic soap and a harsher rubbing down with a hessian 'towel'. Looking back I think the treatment was intended to cure my day-dreaming, but it never did. I went back up to the wee moss but each time I made my way there by a circuitous route, heading for the low bog which lay in the opposite direction, and then circling back behind drystone walls and hedges and travelling round the whole farm to get where I wanted. It was by chance that I was there when the eggs hatched. The duck began to move and her nest-lining was wafted away by the breeze. I heard the peeping of ducklings and then one slithered down the bank and struggled helplessly to try to get up it again. I drew my breath when presently the bank seemed to swarm with brown-dappled, yellow ducklings. The dapples themselves were the colour of the peat. The duck looked about and then moved from the nest. Her ducklings followed in a string, scrambling and falling in their anxiety not to be left behind. The very last of them turned over onto its back, I remember, and cried plaintively but the others went on. After a lot of kicking and struggling the tardy one got back on its keel and paddled its way into the heather stalks. For a moment I saw the complete brood afloat on the waterhole with the duck paddling first with one foot and then the other. She turned and turned again to supervise their progress on the way to the other side. It was a kind of miracle and I desperately hoped that they would all stay there although I knew they wouldn't. They were wild. They didn't belong in any one place and they proved it by going into the weeds and brush beyond the drain.

I never saw them again. The summer never again seemed quite so bright as it had been. I went up two or three times but the water was still mirroring clouds. There wasn't even a feather drifting on its surface, or a footprint on the peat round it. I was filled with gloom but when I finally told one of the men who worked for my grandfather he smiled and said my ducklings were out there in the marshy ground, their dapples protecting them while their feathers grew and they learned to fly in the same way that young grouse took to the air. They would be back, come the back-end of the season when the corn was lying after rain, stuffing themselves and growing fat. In another year, who could say, the duck might be back in that very same place with another brood. Didn't the swallows in the cart shed and the byre come again and the house martins down at Low Malzie? And so the nesting place of the mallard remained in my mind. I was confident that I would see the duck again, and whenever two or three wild duck passed over I was sure my particular bird was among them. That summer when they cut the hay in the next field a cousin who had the same kind of curiosity about things as myself discovered an adder asleep on the bank and without fear pursued it with a cattle drench bottle and a small stick until he forced it to escape from him by going into the bottle. The adder became the focal point of my attention for a while but then came personal disaster. I was whisked up and taken to live with my mother and father on the outskirts of Glasgow. A year or two later I was transported south to live in Middlesex and the serene and beautiful world of my childhood seemed to be on the other side of the world. A curlew cried as it flew over the suburbs and I cried too. I rarely saw a wild duck. When I did I stood in a dream world of my own.

I was thirteen when my grandmother died. Her death was unexpected. She had lived a peaceful, gentle life, harming no one, and perhaps people who live this way are blessed with a peaceful end. The suffering is for those who are left. When my father hurried north for the funeral and took me with him it was decided that, despite the demands of my education, I should stay on to be some sort of comfort for my inconsolable grandfather and my grieving aunts. I was in heaven once again. Grandmother died in the spring of the year when the land was awakening from its winter sleep. Peewits were on the fields, wheeling and crying. Curlews had come up from the water meadows along the river to nest on the moss. With every day that passed the light grew stronger and brighter. My aunts were about their business, churning butter, looking after their poultry and lambing the black-face ewes. I was free to roam as I pleased to find a robin's nest under the mouldboards of an old three-furrow horse-plough, and a wagtail nesting on the burn not far from the stone on which the waterhens had their nest. I wasn't summoned home, nor did I go to Malzie school for even a single day, for I hadn't been enrolled there. The schoolmaster in Middlesex had simply been told that I had been left with the family in Scotland. My education was left to Providence. In May, remembering the mallard on the wee moss, I stood in wonder, in the very same place, to see the duck on her nest. Could it be the same duck, I wondered. I know now that it couldn't possibly have been, and what I had discovered was that marvellous thing, the natural place for a certain species. In a lifetime a man who knows the fields discovers that a hare always rises where he has put up a hare, that for more than a decade partridges have haunted the same bank or knoll, just as a woodcock springs in the same glade and geese keep to the same flight lines through generations. I didn't see the birds leave the nest this time, but being bolder and more confident that I wouldn't get trapped in the peat slough, I went out across the boggy ground and there, scuttling and splashing ahead of me, were half-fledged ducklings while their parent stood far off and watched me. There was something reassuring in all this so far as I was concerned. A poet had said that God was in his heaven and all was right with the world. Things would always be so, unless of course, someone came along and saw personal profit (or subsidy) to be earned by destroying the wilderness, ploughing it up after draining it and banishing birds and animals to which it had belonged. I have never felt that the expediency under which the environment and habitat of wild creatures is altered and renovated is anything but a kind of bloody-minded vandalism, but in this particular place the water-logged waste remained. My grandfather died. I walked round his farm shortly afterwards and a mallard rose from the peat drain where the previous generations of mallard had risen. Years passed. I was grown and married with a family of my own. My aunts had retired to live in a village two or three miles from the place and they died in due course, one when she was seventy-six and the other at eighty-four, which seems to indicate that the hard life of the peasant isn't necessarily a short one.

I attended the funeral of the elder of my two aunts, and that day, at the invitation of the owner of the farm, on which I had been brought up, I went to walk round the fields for the very last time. It just happened to be May. Some features of the landscape had changed. Two woods as well as the dried white stones that used to grow under the plough or the harrows had disappeared. Greed had made the owners of the estate sell the lovely woods. The growing stones had been rolled into the furrows with a heavy water-roller. A hooded crow, a bird hardly ever seen in that part of the world, had nested in a gnarled tree on the fringe of the wee moss. I walked to that corner, almost ruining a pair of new shoes in the process, so that I could look at the water-hole. The breeze bowed the bog cotton and spread the scent of peat and myrtle. I squelched through the porridge of peat. While I was standing there a mallard duck went off going directly into the air with feet trailing before she levelled out and went round. Had she gone directly away, as a frightened bird flushed from a pond of flies, I would have been sadly disappointed. She circled and I smiled happily to myself as I returned to the farm and my car. In half a century this, at least, remained unchanged.

10 THE BIRD-CATCHER

Between summer and the end of autumn we saw increasing numbers of birds that had been nesting along the banks and in the thorn hedges where they had been bred up. First of all it might be a family of greenfinches or linnets, or perhaps a group of young goldfinches flitting along the edge of corn turning from green to yellow as it ripened, or coming happily over a sea of turnips to find perching places along the headland. As time went on the numbers of birds would build up into what would finally become winter flocks that followed one another on migration. The species of birds would change until we were left with our resident chaffinches and the ever-present housesparrows, always attracted by the wind-winnowed chaff heap, by seeds where a hayrick might have been taken down or by corn left in the stackyard after threshing. In the dead of winter, once in a while, there would be snow buntings but, however colourful the snow birds were, my delight was in seeing the goldfinches for they could have been painted by an artist. I still think they are by far the handsomest and most colourful of our native birds, more beautifully coloured than even the bullfinch. We saw few bullfinches however. They didn't often come to pick the blossom from our old apple trees. To see a host of goldfinches all I needed to do was to go over into a neighbour's farm where there was a wilderness field of thistle, teazle, rusty dock and 'gowans'. Here, in what we called the goldfinch field, Scotch thistles were bigger and better than anywhere else for miles. They stood along a ditch on one side of the field as tall as cow parsley with those hollow stalks from which I made peashooters, using hard hawthorn berries for ammunition. I went to the field because it was alongside a burn I liked to fish with a willow stick and a piece of brown line. I would dangle a worm and catch brightly-coloured trout sheltering beneath brambles that hung over the water. Sometimes, when the worm waved in the current behind its anchoring weight and no fish came to investigate, my thoughts would be interrupted by the sound of goldfinches on the field. In the stackyard at home a time came when the chirping and twittering of birds could be heard almost a quarter of a mile away. The result was a kind of bird bedlam. Here, in the goldfinch field, there was a special kind of music and I would leave my line looped round a branch and the 'rod' lying on the bank and go to watch the birds on the thistles. Sometimes the air was filled not only with the sound of the birds but air-borne thistle seeds carried away on the breeze. The goldfinches distributed as much seed as they ate while they perched and fluttered round the heads of those white-haired, over-blown Scotch thistles. If I ventured too near, the birds would spray upwards and whirl off to settle somewhere else, but they never deserted the field. It was their banqueting table until the weeds shrivelled and the field became desolate.

The first encounter I had with the bird-catcher was at the goldfinch field. It was a wonderful day. The water of the burn washed merrily round boulders, carrying the flotsam of the far-away moss onwards, and flexing branches dipped into it like bows strained to fire an arrow.

The sun blessed the field and warmed the earth. Butterflies, the Meadow Brown and the Scotch Argus, were there, flitting from one flower to another and tumbling in mid-air. I was carried away by it all and it was only after I had been day-dreaming for a while that I saw a bird fluttering continually. It wasn't on a thistle but on a dead black-thorn lying among the weeds. There was obviously something wrong. A goldfinch rises and comes down, picks at seedhead, flutters and rises again, but this bird stayed in place. Its fluttering was desperate. It was fastened on the thorn. (I had never come across birdlime, but I knew about it. At least one of the poachers who came about the farm employed it to get pheasants in a particularly wicked way. The noxious substance is made by boiling the bark of a holly tree and mixing it with another substance obtained for a few pennies from a chemist's shop. Bird-catchers and fowlers have made it since the beginning of time I suppose.) The struggling victim was caught in a treacle-like mess plastered all over the thorns. My hands were fouled with the stuff when I freed the bird, but there was something more startling. Down in the weeds was a 'double-deck' cage and an imprisoned goldfinch meant to lure another bird to alight on the roof. The upper cage had a trapdoor to the prison beneath and this was set so delicately that it opened under the slightest pressure the moment a bird fluttered onto the cage. The trap hadn't caught anything as yet but it seemed to me my duty to release the bird in the lower cage. I did this holding the other lime-smeared goldfinch in my free hand. The battered and very frightened decoy flew so fast I hardly saw it go. I retreated from the middle of the field to recover my 'tackle'. I had caught no fish but as I was about to cross the burn there was a commotion on the far side of the field, an angry shouting, and the sudden appearance of an extraordin-ary figure, in a loose black overcoat and an old felt hat. I didn't stop to find out who he was; I knew as I fled that he was the man who had put down the cage trap and smeared the blackthorns with birdlime. He came like a flapping crow that couldn't quite take off. Even a glimpse of him out of the corner of my eye filled me with terror. He wanted his bird. He was furious at my interference. He would flay me alive, he shouted.

Before anyone can be flayed they have to be caught however. A speeding hare was no faster than I was that day. I flew along the bank. I sailed over the burn I had fallen in more than once when I couldn't quite summon the same fleetness of foot. The bird-catcher stormed and swore but his carrion crow's voice faded behind me. I hurried home with the wretched goldfinch in my hand but even holding it with great care didn't improve its condition. It was fouled with lime and no one knew how to cleanse its feathers. The bird-catcher probably had some kind of solvent or antidote, but for once Grandfather was stumped. Although he took the bird away 'to see what he could do' I knew he would return and say it had died. I have no doubt he made a merciful end of it. The bird-catcher came on the scene as a migrant himself, for he didn't belong in the countryside but plied his trade as an itinerant like the tinkers of that day. Setting clap nets and trammel nets as well as using decoys and lures were the operations by which he made his living. The birds were supplied to markets with which he had connections to sing in cages in grubby basements or even in the windows of grand houses in the far off city. It was talk of this cruelty that made both my aunts sentimental about 'tarnished' goldfinches and dejected, rosy-breasted 'linnties' that slumped on perches of 'gilded cages'. Surely the violins played for them as they did for the weeping heroine in the melodramas they sometimes saw in a travelling theatre.

The bird-catcher carried his stock-in-trade lashed to an old bicycle and concealed items in which the policeman might have been interested beneath his long black overcoat. Somewhere he had a temporary base and there he kept his captives in cages or boxes. Once someone who loved birds and detested bird-catchers had taken the law into his own hands and confiscated the entire bag, releasing, it was said, something like three hundred miserable linnets and goldfinches. The police had already had the bird-catcher through their hands, but not for trapping finches. He had stolen a peacock from the grounds of a 'big house'. While bird-catching was frowned upon, stealing an ornamental bird from a laird was something else! The bird-catcher had been sent to prison. The man in the long black coat caught up with me in bed that night for I had a nightmare about him and I knew he would be after me for the rest of my life! I looked for him everywhere in spite of being told that he was really a cowardly individual who would run if challenged. I was too small to confront him and he blighted the summer for me. I hadn't the courage to go back and fish the burn or even think of going into the goldfinch field.

A day came when, instead of the devil in the black overcoat catching up with me, I unwittingly caught up with him. I was sitting in the gig, 'happy as a sand boy' looking over drystone walls and thornhedges lining the road and paying little attention to the road ahead. Grandfather was driving. An aunt was with us and she was singing to herself as she often did on these occasions. All at once I saw a figure on a bicycle a little way ahead. The flapping overcoat and the hunched outline told me who it was. My throat contracted. I was terrified again. The gear slung on it made the bicycle wobble and sway as the loose chain was cranked by the bird-catcher's large ill-fitting boots. Once he gave us a backward glance to make sure he wasn't going to be run down, and he might have been, for Grandfather recognized him. In the ordinary way the old man would give anyone the road and the time of day. Sometimes he would slow the pony and hold a conversation that would last for a mile or so, but the bird-catcher was not a person he had time for. He kept the gig on a straight line until the man riding the old bike was pushed onto the verge. Everything tumbled in a heap and the wheels of his machine remained in the air. The bird-catcher gave out a string of oaths. My aunt, who had stopped singing, shook a small, hard flat fist and told him that he was a wicked man. Grandfather didn't even look round and behaved as though there had been no one there in the first place. I glanced back. I saw the bird-catcher in his rage and it didn't comfort me in the least. I was sure he was staring at me, remembering where he had seen me before. 'That man,' said my aunt, 'should be locked up in the jile!' She wasn't in the least sorry at what had happened to him. She would have had him in prison. She was a great sentimental-ist about little birds, as everyone knew, but she was also furious that this character had given me a nightmare.

We came to harvest that year with a succession of glorious days when stubbles were warm and fragrant and partridges that seemed like miniature fowl travelled over. The stackyard was filled with well-thatched, round ricks of hay, oats and barley to be used for feed or threshed out for the distillery. The old chaff heaps were raked and burned. There was only the potato crop to be harvested before turnips were brought in. The fields were full of birds in assorted parties: twites and greenfinches as light as thistledown themselves, the inevitable chaffinches that stayed through the winter, and hosts of sparrows to glean wherever corn or wild seed had fallen. The bird-catcher took his own harvest. I didn't see him or hear of him from any of the casuals who came to gather the potatoes. No one belonging to the family mentioned him and I didn't know his name. I don't think anyone knew his real name but he was universally disliked, a pariah as bad as a sheep-worrying dog or a landlord who turned a family out in winter. Any kind of name was too good for such an animal, my aunt once said. Even in her worst fits of indignation she couldn't find a word that expressed her contempt for the bird-catcher. I was depressed by being reminded of him. He had become the personification of a bogey man. I dared not think of him in case my food became solid in my stomach and my mind scuttled like a mouse played with by a cat. All these bouts of horror were prompted by the thought of the man in the long black coat lumbering after me like a giant crow, ten times the size of the smithy raven and a thousand times more terrifying. I told one of my grandfather's men just how frightened I was, and he promised to find the devil for me and put the fear of God in him so badly that he would never show his face in the countryside again, but by the very nature of his business the bird-catcher was a hard man to find. He skulked in thickets and lay behind dikes or hedges waiting for birds to fall to his lures, become entangled in his nets, or trapped in birdlime. I didn't expect the ploughman to find him, and he didn't, but I was quite sure that had the paths of the two men crossed the bird-catcher would have got his come-uppance if only to prove the ploughman was loyal to his employer. Harm one of us, we were fond of saying, and you harm us all.

In the winter, when the bird-catcher was far away, I managed to forget him. He was probably busy netting bushes and old ricks in his own part of the country to get birds for a sparrow pie. But the winter passed. Spring and peesweeps came again. The yellowhammer sang and the lark ascended and plumetted like a falling stone when it had done spiralling upwards. I began to go to the burns to fish and went down to the smithy after rain, for that was always the time to get trout on the worm, the smith had told me, while all that food was washing downstream and the trout were waiting behind every boulder to take it. One day I was on the footpath looking down the road that led to the smithy. I was dismayed to see my nightmare character wheeling his loaded bicycle up the slope. I approached the signpost. He seemed an eternity coming and looked even more sinister than before as he pushed the bike with his coat sweeping the ground. I was afraid he would look up and see me there on the side of the footpath, crouching behind the whin bush, but he didn't. He looked at the road the way a weary man does with one foot going in front of the other as though the journey will never end. I could see his lips moving for he talked to himself. I prayed he wouldn't look up and spot me, but I needn't have worried. He turned at the signpost and went on up the Alticry road without looking left or right. I could hear the rattle and jangle of loose mudguards and other bits and pieces of his ancient bike and waited until even the sound diminished before I stepped through the gate onto the public road to go down to the smithy. I looked back several times to make sure he hadn't changed his mind and was retracing his steps. The smith saw the strained look on my face and asked me what it was all about. I told him. He laughed. Hadn't I faced worse than that miserable character, Soldier Scott for example, that hero of the Great War, on sentry go at the signpost and mad as any March hare at the best of times, and madder still at full moon? But 'Soger' Scott was only shell-shocked and harmless except when afflicted by nightmares of the Somme or wherever he had been. The bird-catcher was wicked, malevolent, the Minister said. He haunted me and he would never go away. I knew it for he had come back again. When I left the smithy I was frightened to go quickly and put distance between me and it, and then couldn't run fast enough to the safety of the footpath to the farm. I had another nightmare that night. My aunts said the policeman should move the bird-catcher right out of the shire, but they must have known this was a forlorn hope. The days passed and the terror diminished until I was happy again.

There might have been no end to this story. The bird-catcher could have been an eternal terror consolidating a neurosis that blighted my life, but most stories have an ending. It was the smith who put the final seal on it all although I couldn't believe it at the time. It wasn't a fishing day when I went down to the smithy on this particular occasion. The sun was bright. The water low. Birds were singing and the house martins that nested at Low Malzie farm were flying in and out of the steading and catching flies. I was on an errand to get some kind of smithy tool my grandfather needed for the repair of an implement. It was I suppose a particular article his own collection of tools, kept since his days at that trade, lacked. I idled along, looking for a waterhen I had seen running towards the roadside pool and peering into a thick thorn to find the nest of a bird that had escaped my attention on some previous occasion. I loved finding even old, long-abandoned nests of grass and horsehair and feathers, or lovely works of lichen and moss woven into thorns. Even the old smooth mud bowl of the thrush's nest delighted me. I was carried away by my day-dreams and these things, when, all at once, there he was, at my shoulder, grabbing my arm, the monster with the hooked nose and the hard hawk-like face. He had caught me at last! I screamed but no sound seemed to come. I felt his fingers biting into my shoulder and I thought my end had come, but I had forgotten the smith. By a miracle he, too, had come along unawares and all at once I was free. The bird-catcher was staggering and his old bike being trundled along with him to the forge! How the smith could curse when the mood took him. Even his raven hadn't heard some of the oaths he used. At the bridge the bird-catcher was dumped on his backside. His bike was swung in the air and went sailing into the deepest part of the burn and vanished. Before the bird-catcher was properly on his feet the smith had popped into the smithy and come out again with a length of red-hot iron drawn from the coals. The bird-catcher ran for his life.

'If I ever see you pass, let alone putting a hand on this wee boy,' the smith yelled, 'I will put hot iron on you! Mind you that!'

The dejected crow of a man went up past the schoolhouse and then on up the road until he was lost from sight. The smith stared after him, still filled with rage.

'He'll not be back,' he promised me.

He was right. The bike and all its dangling appendages gathered grass and other debris until a flood shifted it on and on downstream; the wretched cages, the matted nets and the birdlime were swallowed up and the bird-catcher finally became as unreal as a character from Grimms' Fairy Tales.

11 THE PIGEON LOFT

When my father was sixteen he was sent off to Glasgow to take up an engineering apprenticeship which his father had managed to get him. Before he obtained his School Leaving Certificate Father had left no one in any doubt about his determination to be an engineer. I doubt very much whether he knew exactly what engineering involved beyond using machinery and fashioning things to a drawing. His father had demonstrated what could be done with iron and made all kinds of agricultural implements, some of them his own invention but the boy knew there were many things a man at a forge couldn't do. A 'smith' rarely had a lathe or did anything to limits less than an eighth of an inch one way or the other. It was this aspect of the engineering trade that made him want to learn. He could easily enough have stayed at home, worked as a clerk in the county buildings and indulged his passion for homing pigeons. He already had a loft of 'doos' as they are called in Scotland – the word is obviously an abbreviation of dove – and they were the delight of his young life, but the magnet of Clydeside, an engineering firm in Govan, drew him, despite his anguish at parting with the family and his birds. Soon, having suffered the awful pangs of homesickness, he was to abscond and return home and dally in the green field where his loft was situated to watch his birds sailing in the bright sunlight. The contrast between the kind of world he had left and the one to which he had newly returned can hardly be described. He had been living in the grime of the city and clatter of a workshop where men in overalls tended their machines and shouted obscenities at one another. He came back to the smoking chimneys of a sleepy town where old men sat in the sun and dogs lay on pavement flags. In the town square the only sound to be heard was the cawing of rooks and the churring of starlings enjoying the warmth of the day. His 'doos' swept over the old stone building of the county gaol and circled the town before coming back to the loft. God was in his heaven for at least a day, and then, his bag repacked and his pigeons having settled to preen or doze, he was escorted by the whole family, back to the train for Glasgow. Everyone except Grandfather cried as the train took that wistful youngster away. He was to be there for seven years. Two years were added to his apprenticeship time as a punishment for taking part in a 'mechanics prank' that might have led to a shipwreck in the Clyde. The loft was neglected. His birds fell prey to natural enemies or farmers who defended their crops with a gun. Worse than this the whole family flitted! Grandmother had had a dairy and kept cows on rented fields. She had also reared other livestock, a few pigs and some poultry, in preparation for the move to the 180 acre farm which Grandfather had leased. Home was no longer a little stone house in Lower Main Street with the Catholic priest as neighbour. It was a farmhouse, not only remote from the town, but out of sight of the public road and without near neighbours. Here the family were to stay for forty years and here Grandfather and Grandmother were to live out their time.

Most young men end up by putting down roots of their own and setting up a home away from the family in which they have been brought up. Father was soon courting mother and getting a home together. When soon after I was born it was decided that I needed the fresh, clean air of the country in order to survive, I was brought down to Galloway and handed over to my grandparents. Father and Mother visited when they could, but not as often as they would have liked because a younger sister was stricken with sleeping sickness and had to be nursed. Father had never abandoned his dream of keeping pigeons but what excuse had he for making a loft at the farm when he wouldn't be there to watch the birds each morning as they flew out? I needed to have pets, he said, it wasn't enough that I had a sheepdog for guardian, a tame duck, a rabbit and a rabbit hutch to keep it in. The rabbit did nothing but munch oatmeal, tea leaves, clover and dandelion. The duck, well a duck didn't fly out every morning and go skimming round the stackyard, did it? One way or another most of us live at second hand, and father's plan for a pigeon loft didn't really involve too much work. Adjoining the byre gable was the gable of the calf house. There was a loft above the snug quarters in which young calves were nursed. What was more, there were two drain tiles already set in the stonework of the gable to ventilate the loft. These red clay drains were wired to stop birds coming in and filling the loft with nesting material, as starlings and jackdaws sometimes do, but the wire could be removed and a box fixed on the wall so that pigeons could drop onto it, pop inside, and find their way into the loft through the drain tiles. I can remember Father spending his holiday fixing the box to the gable and then putting wire netting on a frame he constructed between the floor and the rafters at the end of the loft. Having done this he made nestboxes. All that he needed were some 'doos'.

To be sure that homers would home to the loft it was necessary to confine the first pair of pigeons until they had young. On a second visit Father brought the pair of birds. They were the handsomest pigeons I had ever seen, blue with flecks of white on their backs and wings. The exit from the loft was closed and I was carried up the ladder to see 'my' birds in their quarters. Anyone who came up was warned that if the trapdoor was thrown back and the birds escaped that would be the last we would ever see of them. They would fly back to Glasgow as fast as they could for they belonged in a loft beside a grim tenement building and the man who had sold them would be delighted to get them back! I couldn't quite believe this. Why would birds want to go back to the dirty city? I had been there and couldn't think why people, let alone birds that could fly free, ever wanted to live there! Father prevailed upon the elder of his two sisters to perform the daily chore of tending the 'doos'. Aunt Mary had enough on her hands, what with pigs and poultry, not to mention her milking stint night and morning, without becoming nursemaid to pigeons, but father was very persuasive and anything that was supposed to be good for me my aunt supported. The pair of doos duly mated and produced their pigeon pair. I was taken to see the youngsters. They were ugly, I remember, and hairy. They looked as though they would never fly. Father came back and satisfied himself that it was safe to open the loft. Both birds flew out and perched on the ridge. Their wings, he explained, were stiff and in need of exercise. It would be a while before they took a real flight. The young birds grew and fledged, and their parents stayed, going in and out of the loft to them and roosting there at night. Pigeons on the ridge attracted first one stray and then another until seven or eight birds began using the loft. This was probably because of the liberal amount of Indian corn and peas my aunt provided for them. The whole flock was known as 'the boy's doos'. Some of them were red checkers and one day a white bird arrived making me greatly excited, but the newcomer didn't stay and went off before evening. Sometimes the flock built up and then diminished again. Grandfather told me that some were bound to be shot on corn. Even the real homers my father had bought in Glasgow were in danger of being led into trouble by feral birds that regularly fed on arable fields.

When father came back a second time he brought yet another pair of birds and the loft had to be partitioned to confine the newcomers and let the resident birds come and go. The new birds were brick-coloured, bright eyed, smart little birds. I could see the difference between feral 'stock' and these carefully-bred homers even when I was barely five years old. The chore of getting up the ladder and feeding the doos became mine now. Every day I would get a ration of pigeon corn and mount the ladder, being careful about the way I lifted the trapdoor. One day as I did this, I found myself looking not at a bird on the floor of the loft but at a beady-eyed grey rat. The rat had killed one of the newly fledged squeakers. I went down the ladder as fast as I could to find a stick to kill the rat. I was furious and wanted that rat dead! When I found what I needed, a big stick used to stir the calves' meal and drink, I clambered back up to the loft, hurriedly dropped the trapdoor and rushed at the rat, but the rat had seen it all before. He scampered into a corner between the slates and the stone wall and slipped away through a hole. I waited for him to show his face again, but he didn't. After several minutes I decided he had gone for good and went back down. At mid-day, when Grandfather and his men were having their meal, I told them how I had put a rat to flight after it had murdered one of my birds. To my dismay they told me the rat would be back. It might have already returned and killed the remaining cheeper. I left the kitchen as fast as my legs would carry me. The adult birds were cooing and strutting along the ridge. I couldn't understand why they weren't in the loft seeing the rat off! I grabbed the 'spurtle' once again and scrambled up the ladder to see what I could do about the rat and once again I met him face to face.

Desperation got me into the loft without falling off the rickety old ladder and the rat took the wrong turning. He ran to the opposite wall and there wasn't a hole he could slip through. I lashed out with the stick and hit him again and again. He was dead before I realised he was incapable of running anywhere. I remember the way his black eyes stared brightly up at me and the blood on his head and his back. Later in life I was told that a cornered rat will spring and attack but I didn't know this at the time. If the rat did come towards me I was flailing with the stick and didn't appreciate what it would have meant had he reached me. There were feathers and sawmill chippings everywhere. My hair was covered in both. I remember I picked up the rat by the tail and slithered down through the trap door. I hadn't bothered to check whether the second squeaker had been killed or not. All I could think was that I had destroyed the rat! A small boy doesn't think of the danger he may be in. Experience educates him. I was only half way to the ground when my foot slipped and I lost my hold and came crashing down. I didn't cry. My breath must have been knocked out of me. When I came round I was being carried back to the kitchen. The rat, the first thing I thought about as we went through the door, had fallen from my hand. I mumbled tearfully and asked someone if they had found it, but no one had seen it. My triumph turned to disappointment. Instead of being praised for killing the rat I was lectured about swarming up and down from the loft every five minutes. No one could imagine what my father had been thinking about when he built the thing and left a 'wean' to disturb the poor birds on their nests. It was foolish, and a manifest folly at that! My bruises were examined, my cuts and grazes treated with iodine. I was told not to go up to the loft again or it would be nailed up! I could have been killed. What would my aunts have said to my mother and father if I had been? I didn't know. I didn't care. I wasn't sorry for myself. I didn't like being settled in the armchair with a rag soaked in vinegar on my brow, whatever it was supposed to do for me!

That same day I watched one of Grandfather's men go up into the loft to make it rat-proof with galvanised sheeting and mortar. After he had done this the ladder was carried off and stowed in the rafters of the cart shed. The pigeons, I was told, would be fed with the hens who also had a ration of Indian corn. Whatever happened in the nestboxes in the loft I wouldn't be going up there by myself again. The kind of hazards farm children face are too numerous to mention. I once nearly vanished in the dung midden; my cries, and the barking of a dog were heard but my rescue was delayed because my head was all there was showing above the mire and it looked like a muddy turnip.

The family weren't being harsh but simply removing a hazard, as Grandfather had done when he saw that I might stray into the corn when it was being harvested. He had a special seat fitted on the binder so that I could ride with him, out of the way of the knives and the plodding hooves of massive horses.

If I was much too young to manage a loft to breed my birds in by pairing them off, I could still admire them flying free. I loved to see them drifting in with their wings outspread as they prepared to land with sunlight showing through their primary feathers. I loved the clatter of take-offs and landings. The cooing when cock birds made up to hens on the ridge was a kind of music. In addition to all this was the colour. A contrast of black and white, red, blue and fawn. I counted the flock and lost count before I was half way through. I walked among them when they were down feeding with the hens. If I knew little or nothing about the proper homing birds, I loved pigeons. It didn't matter whether they were true-bred or the strain of feral birds a fancier would call runts. The presence of the 'doos' was taken for granted by the household. Once in a while, after sowing or when young corn was sprouting, Grandfather said something would have to be done about them. He said the same thing about the guinea fowl in their turn, but one day something dramatic happened. From away up in the heavens a peregrine came plummetting down. I had never seen a falcon before. This was a well-keepered countryside. Hawks of any kind were destroyed either in the nest, if things got that far, or with traps, guns and poisoned baits. Everything that was a threat to game was put down. Every snake was an adder of course! The falcon must have been a passage bird searching for a mate and territory in which to breed or had come down from the Galloway hills to hunt pigeons. All at once one of my birds was knocked out of the air and the falcon was up and away. Nothing remained to show what had happened but three or four small feathers drifting on the breeze. I hurried indoors to tell someone. Ah, they said, the old hawk was here, was he? There were too many pigeons on the roof. If he took half a dozen I would never miss them. There would be more corn for those that remained. I didn't want to lose a single bird. They were mine and I loved them but in the afternoon it happened again. This time the pigeon wasn't taken but it was struck so hard that it fluttered down into the stackyard and perched on a hawthorn tree, its eyes half-closed and its head slowly drooping. I couldn't reach it. Before the afternoon was out it toppled from the branch. I found it dead in the long grass. I cried for it and then took it off and buried it in the field. I looked for the peregrine and didn't see him, but the following day he was back again and killed another bird.

'So long as it is only taking a few wild pigeons,' Grandfather said, 'it isn't doing much harm. It catches the slow and the weak ones. Your best ones are fast and get away.' That was no consolation so far as I was concerned. I was sorry for the weak and the slow ones. I hoped the keeper might come and put a shot behind the falcon. He always threatened to do this to farm dogs when he spotted them 'poaching'. My flock diminished but there was nothing that could be done. Even if Grandfather had agreed to shoot the 'old hawk' he couldn't stand about all day waiting for it to stoop on a pigeon. I needn't have worried, however. The falcon killed his quota and in a few days the doos were settling on the roof, no longer nervous and frightened of a bolt from the blue. Father came and went. There was talk of my going 'home' now.

My young sister had died and I was now sturdy and strong. My grandparents took me up to Glasgow on a visit but I refused to stay. Although they took me back with them my mother insisted I had to be rescued from the 'wild' life of the farm. There must be an end to indulgence of my every whim and I couldn't be allowed to moon my days away, learning nothing, watching birds and fishing. That kind of life might be alright for a Huckleberry Finn. It wouldn't do for her son! Leaving my 'doos' was only part of the trauma of going to live in a shipbuilding town but I was hardly there before Father's plans to avoid the consequences of the slump by finding employment down in England bore fruit. We were soon away to a foreign land. I would see the dawn coming up in the Midlands, patchworks of allotments as we neared the city, and a dreary flatness along the Thames. We settled finally in a newly built house with a 'garden' that was really a builders tip for buried in it was all the rubbish bricklayers, plasterers, carpenters and plumbers had managed to gather together. The world had gone wrong for me. The only thing that brightened my day was the flight of homers from a loft behind some cottages at the end of the road. The man who kept the loft let me stand and watch while he released his birds. He showed me how to handle a pigeon and examine its spread wing, and how the pigeon trap works. He was the first real fancier I ever met but his neighbours said he wasted his substance on birds and beer. On Saturdays he would stand, swaying on his feet, watching pigeons flying until, in the end, quite overcome by drink, he fell down and lay there sleeping. My mother didn't approve of my visiting the loft and my father wasn't very pleased at the company I seemed determined to keep. He decided I must have pigeons of my own. We went North for a holiday and came back again with a pair of birds to establish a loft. The birds were descendants of the first birds Father had bought. While he considered how he could have his aviary and I my pigeon loft, the 'doos' were kept in a small enclosure knocked up from boxes and wire-netting. My pigeons seemed perfectly happy even although they weren't let out. Once they bred, Father said again, everything would be alright. I could have a proper loft and start to breed my own birds. This dream came to nothing for one day I discovered that the door of the enclosure had sprung open. The birds were nowhere to be seen. They hadn't joined the fancier's flock. He checked his trap for me, and shook his head. 'You know where they are now?' he asked. 'More than halfway to Scotland, maybe even there already.' A week later we had a letter from Grandfather. The birds were on the ridge. They were homers and had flown three hundred miles to get back. The improvised pigeon shed was taken apart and I never had the chance to start again. My 'doos' fly in my imagination, back there in the world of my childhood. I can see them yet.

12 THE SECRET ROOKERY

Two things fill me with nostalgia for my childhood. One is the sound of a cock crowing on a bright summer's morning and the other the happy cawing of rooks as they leave the trees and fly out over the countryside to forage for food. The cock crow always made me stand and listen for some other cockerel replying, a bird on the midden of another farm. The countryside was so peaceful in those days. There was no background hum of a tractor ploughing or an articulated vehicle droning along with a stack of fertiliser large enough to cover all the farms in sight. If there was any sound to be heard it was the bleating of lambs or the lowing of a heifer, perhaps the creaking of a cart axle or the thuds of someone knocking in a fence-post. Cock crow carried a very long way and I would amuse myself deciding just whose cockerels were replying. The rooks – they were all 'ciaws' whether they were bald on the beak or not – would rise in a cloud above the smithy rookery at around ten in the morning and mill around for minutes before setting their course for wherever they had decided to go. This was another fascinating thing. The rooks didn't follow the same route or flight line as the geese did in winter, but they had some kind of discussion while they circled and the idlers among them skirmished with one another. Watching them from a distance, I would see them drifting like smoke in a breeze and then heading out over a particular farm. They would gain height and go on with excited cawing that obviously meant something. Two or three birds always seemed to influence the rest about which way they should go. Later in life when we talked about the rook behaviour my grandfather said there was something special about it. Rooks decided where they would get the food they wanted but why did they ignore one field and go to another? Often both fields had the same crop. Watching them flying I would see them ignoring old so-and-so's rootfield but heading for a slope a mile or two farther away. Another day their flight would be to a field they had ignored before. Some old farmers believed that a curse was on them when the rooks came swirling and tumbling down to their well-weeded and well-thinned swedes to begin tearing the young plants out. It seemed as though the black birds were malignant. They pulled the plant but didn't eat it and left it lying there wilting in the sun. Re-sowing was never any use. By the time new seed germinated it was too late, it had to be ready for October when swedes were always topped and carted home for the standing-in-herd. A curse they were, the old people said, inflicted by some enemy who had the way of such things! Their ravaged field advertised what the 'ciaws' had done from the day it was devastated until the few turnips left on it were lifted and carted.

The rookery beyond the smithy was one of the most fascinating places I visited. I could spend hours there in spring and early summer. I often did, because it flanked a dam from which a sluice ran to the waterwheel used to power the smithy gear. I would settle by the dam to fish with a worm and listen to the rooks about their business. How buoyantly they could float above a nest or hover above a hungry, half-fledged nestling. Rooks have a positively buoyant flight, lighter than the carrion crow, and they are gregarious. They love one another's company. They have a way of plaguing, teasing and irritating one another that is wonderful to watch. In spring the way they quarrel over sticks and occupy themselves plaguing a neighbour always reminds me of quarrelling villagers who live as close to one another as rooks. Sometimes, locked together, a pair of birds would come tumbling, over and over, right down to the ground. I once saw a pair fall on the water and get carried by the current to the lip of the dam. Here one drowned but the other, after a pitiful struggle, got to the end of the barrier and safely into the grass. Whether it got back into the air or not I didn't discover. I was on the other side of the water perched on a dead tree that had toppled into the dam and I was fishing with a line threaded through between my big toe and the one next to it, in order to keep clear of snags in the water. I remember an eel taking the worm and the rough brown line searching my toes before I freed myself and let the eel wind itself round something under the water. All the time this was going on the rooks kept up their clamour in the high tops of the trees and whitened the nettles down in the wood below with spatterings of lime. I would watch them and forget the passing of time until my eyes became dazed by the black silhouettes of trees and nests and the brilliance of a sunlit sky beyond. I loved this place: a few fallen sticks, a greeny-fawn eggshell or just a black primary feather filled me with delight. The whole world seemed wonderful and I would come out of the wood stimulated as much as a modern child who has been watching a science fiction film.

A time comes when young rooks flap out of their nest and learn how to get about in the twigs and branches that surround it. Encouraged by their parents they try to fly into the tops of the adjoining trees but, because they haven't developed either the muscle or the agility to keep them airborne, they find themselves perching in lower and lower branches. Occasionally, scolded by their parents who flap round in great anxiety, they reach the ground. Rooks become particularly agitated when this happens because predators of one sort or another may lurk in the undergrowth. Cats will seize a young rook. A fox may slip out and make off with a meal. Even a hedgehog will munch on a helpless bird. There were no foxes anywhere near the smithy wood but there were a great many cats around it and the adjoining cottages. A stoat or even a weasel would make an end of a rook given the chance. The cawing and flapping of the parents often draws attention to the youngster. This happened one day when I was happily dangling a worm in the dam, hoping a really big trout would find it in the silt. I watched a pair of rooks continually flying down to a patch of nettles and then perching forlornly on a branch immediately above. I let the worm fend for itself, went up the burn to a safe crossing place and came down on the other side to search for the young rook. I found the fledgling among the nettles looking just the way it must have looked in the nest. I picked it up but it showed a determination not to be handled by pecking my hand and taking hold of the skin. I let it keep its hold while we went back over the burn. Its parents flew out of the trees, swooped on me, cawed frantically, and infected the whole rookery with the same kind of panic. Birds flapped and flew everywhere. I was afraid they would mob me. They didn't, but the parents of the fledgling swept close to my head and made a lot of noise. I tucked the young rook inside my jacket and left. I had found myself a pet and I had the old rabbit hutch to keep it in. My big black and white rabbit had died without showing the slightest sign of being unwell and the hutch had become vacant.

No one at home had any time for crows. Even the raven was considered a wicked self-indulgence on the part of the smith. All hawks were enemies to the keeper and all black birds were enemies of the farmer. Someone would always have to spend days 'herding' them off the potato field when the crop was ready for lifting. In spring scarecrows were made for the turnip fields and fields of young corn. Harbouring an enemy was unthinkable! I knew what they would say, but I innocently hoped the young rook in the rabbit hutch would escape notice. I planned to feed it with worms from the garden and titbits of food and hoped it wouldn't advertise itself by cawing. It was just possible that, having so much to do, no one would even glance at the old green, algaed rabbit hutch in the corner by the black shed. I managed to get the fledgling housed without anyone noticing and spent an hour getting worms for him. The first one I fed him almost choked him and I had to pull it back out of his throat. The worm was too big and too lively for even a hungry rook and so I found a knife to chop it up with; for a small bird he took an awful lot of chopped worm, then blinked once or twice, closed his eyes and went to sleep. I left him to it. The family didn't seem to have noticed anything, but then one of my aunts, who had been to the garden for something asked me what I had been digging for. The worms round the midden were better for fishing, weren't they? I was lost for an explanation. I said I thought maybe bigger worms would catch bigger fish.

The young rook settled down in a day and opened his beak for food whenever I came near the hutch, but then he began to call a lot. To my dismay I saw two black birds flapping round the black shed. I couldn't imagine they were his parents. The whole crow tribe has a tendency to get worked up about any of their kind in trouble. Even a newly-shot crow will bring others to the scene to lament, sometimes for an hour. I knew this from Willie, who had the job of keeping crows away from crops with the old gun. He would shoot a crow and lay it out, spread-eagled, and then conceal himself so that he could shoot its relatives. In a little while those crows flapping round the hutch would be noticed! I hurried to put them to flight. They sailed round and came back to complain louder than before. The bird in the hutch replied with its own pitiful complaint and there was nothing I could do. While the two birds were flying round my new-found pet refused to take bits of worm. Inevitably the family discovered what was going on.

'I knew you were up to something!' my aunt said when she found the bird in the hutch. 'Think shame on yourself! You talked about getting worms for fishing and catching big fish with big worms. You kenned very well you were telling lies!'

I was ashamed of myself and I was forgiven. The hutch was no place for the crow they told me. The place for it was where it belonged, in a tree. If it came pulling turnips the place for it was tied by the feet to a stick to warn its brothers and sisters what they would get if they kept coming! I pleaded for the young rook, but in vain. If it could fly well enough to go back to where it came from the hutch door would be left open. If it couldn't fly well enough to get down to the smithy I was to take it back there. Just because the smith kept a raven I wasn't to think I could keep any crow that came near enough for me to grab it.

I knew the unfortunate fledgling couldn't possibly fly back to its rookery and there was nothing else for me to do but take it back. I had already been sent back with a young partridge I had caught, and marched back to restore a half-fledged chaffinch (a shilfie) to its nest. Mournfully I carried the young rook back to the smithy wood. On the way I met the smith who examined it and shrugged his shoulders. Well, it might manage to survive, he said, but before the week was out there would be hardly any young rooks in the wood. I was putting it back to have it killed. The 'gentlemen' farmers came every year at this time to shoot young rooks in the treetops. It kept the colony down. It saved shot. They used small-bore rifles. The old birds flew out and all but the newly-fledged ones were executed one after another. They were not much more than sitting targets. The shooters gathered the birds and cut the breast meat off to make rook pie.

I took my wretched young rook into the wood and released it but it didn't fly up into the trees and settled in brambles where it was spotted by adult birds who immediately began cawing and flapping down to it. I retreated, hoping that sooner or later its proper parents might find it.

The smith said I had probably filled it with so many bits of worm it simply couldn't fly. The following day just after the clock had chimed twelve I heard shooting down at the rookery, the short, sharp report of what we called pea rifles, .22 guns the rook shooters used. Occasionally there was the heavier bang of a twelve bore and my aunts shook their heads. They had no time for crows but they didn't like wanton killing.

'That wee craw of yours will be dead by now, son', they said. 'You couldn't save it either bringing it here or leaving it where it was.'

I knew they were right. The following day I went down to the smithy to fish. The nettles were trampled. The wood was strangely silent. There wasn't a bird anywhere. The adult rooks had forsaken the place, disturbed by what had happened. I was saddened by the sight of so many mutilated corpses and feathers and blood strewn in the under-growth. It had been a great day for killing rooks. Looking back at my life I am glad that although I have done more than my share of killing I never did take part in an organised rook shoot. The old rookery was silent for the rooks lived away from it for a while. I often wondered why they didn't abandon the place and make a rookery somewhere else, and then, years later, when I was at the farm one spring I discovered that they had established a kind of satellite rookery, a new base. I suppose it happened because they were persecuted too often and a natural adjustment took place. I discovered the secret rookery quite by chance. I am sure no one else except the keeper, perhaps, knew it was there in the low planting, a block of spruce with one or two decidious trees that stood inside the boundary of the farm. That rooks nested there would have agitated Grandfather before he came to the conclusion that their turnip pulling wasn't wilful and they weren't attacking the plant but pulling it up to get at a fat, slug-like grub we called a pout. The pout, which I never saw but only heard about, attacked the root of the swede the way the grub of the cabbage fly bores into the root of a cabbage plant and makes it wilt. Grandfather and one or two of his neighbours finally came to see that the uprooted swedes were already doomed. The rook, with an instinct for something particularly nourishing, pulled the plants out to get the grub. When they didn't find one they moved on, pulled another and yet another. This didn't stop the war against the crow, rook or carrion-eater, of course.

I took credit for discovering the rookery no one ever thought existed. Watching the rooks going away from the smithy wood one morning I saw the direction they were taking. When, perhaps ten minutes later, rooks seemed to climb into the sky from behind the low planting I was puzzled. I couldn't think how they would have got there. I waited until the happy train of birds went on over our hill to a farm beyond it and then I went down to the low planting. Crows had roosted there overnight it seemed and perhaps they did that every night. It was almost as exciting as finding the route a corncrake takes to its nest. I crawled under the old rusty barbed wire that was fastened to thorn trees on the boundary and made my way into the shadowy silent plantation. In the thicker part larches and an odd Scots pine or two crowded one another so closely that at ground level there was only room for me to go on hands and knees. Clustered in the thick mass of branches aloft I discovered not just an odd nest of sticks but a whole colony of rooks! Here was a secret rookery where every year a new generation of rooks grew up unmolested by the rook shooters who visited the smithy wood. I could hardly believe it, but excited though I was I told no one at home. I thought they might insist on clearing out the rooks to keep them from the fields. Later I climbed one of the spruce trees in a positive rain of crumbled twigs and bark debris to get to the nests. There were dozens of these. In the first I came to I found a page from the *Scottish Farmer*, a paper Grandfather always read as soon as the postman brought it. It bore that year's date. It had probably been used to wrap the plough-man's piece and then a rook had picked it from the furrow for nest material.

In the spring of the following year I managed to get to the planting and climbed from one tree top into the next to look into the cluster of nests built closer together than rooks ever built in the smithy wood. I didn't tell anyone about the rookery but eventually I shared my secret with my younger brother. He, incidentally, made several ascents until, as he was nearing the top of one of the tall spruce poles the dead branches on which he put his foot gave way. All at once he found himself coming down, the weight of his body and his increasing momentum breaking every branch until he hit the ground. The floor of the wood was a bed of deep mould and dry conifer needles. He was unhurt but he wouldn't go up again, and neither did I. The years passed. I spent most of them away in Middlesex. The farm passed into new hands. I called once to look round and was saddened to see that not only had the secret rookery gone, but the whole plantation, with the exception of a dead tree or two, had been felled. There was a carrion crow perched on one of the dead trees. Its call was harsh and nothing like the happy sound the rooks used to make.

13 SINGING BIRDS

My mother told me once that, had she realised what it was going to lead to, she would have put something in the drinking water of the first canary my father had. It was a bird to brighten the sombre world in which he earned his living. It sang late and early and hung in a silvered, if not golden cage, in the living room. When Father wanted to make it sing in pure ecstasy, he would open the living-room door and then the bathroom door and run all the taps. The bright little canary would sing like Caruso and father would sit, smiling and listening, to the endless song. I suppose it harked back to his country upbringing. Mother, being bred up in a town, didn't really appreciate the sound, but of course she would never have poisoned the poor bird. She, like my father really, had a very tender heart for small and helpless creatures. The possession of one singing bird didn't satisfy father, however. He would have two, and two cages! He would make his own cages and have them snug but roomy. He would get mates for both his singing birds. He would breed a few more birds and make presents of them to his friends. Finally, he would get a cage for a very special bird which he would take as a present for my grandmother. At about this time he had had another hobby, the construction of wireless sets, not those everyday crystal sets some people were tinkering with because the wireless was the coming thing, but what were called tube sets, great desk-like affairs adorned with moving coils and brass terminals to set off bulbous 'valves'. His success as a wireless buff prompted Father to take the first wireless set down into his native district. He would put up a very tall aerial and his father and mother would be amazed when they listened to the experimental station he listened to in Glasgow. Unfortunately, the hills were against Father. The wireless signal was too weak at that time for it to be heard in such a remote area. Some people laughed behind Father's back and said he wasn't quite as clever as he thought himself to be. Well, if he was ahead of his time in radio, he could breed a prize canary and bring that to hang in his father's house! None of the farmers round about had a singing canary.

I happened to be there when the present was brought. The journey was a difficult one for Mother and Father, travelling with their usual luggage plus a canary. The bird was protected from draughts in the train by a wrapping of brown paper. They all arrived safely and the cage was unveiled. The poor bird which had fluttered itself into near exhaustion couldn't get up on the perch, let alone whistle or sing. It sat dejectedly on a bed of sand and couldn't be coaxed onto the perch. It looked as though Father had another non-starter. The canary's virility was questioned. Crouched on the floor of its cage it looked more like a hen than a singing cock. It took no seed. It ignored the water in the drinker. Finally, when everyone had looked at it, it was hoisted aloft and the cage hung from a hook above Grandfather's chair. Most of the family doubted that it would ever become used to the smoke from the old man's pipe for he burned an ugly, strong-smelling black twist. Grandmother consoled Father. The bird had to get used to the kitchen. It would come to and take nourishment. She had no doubt of that. Father went off round the fields to have his cobwebs blown away and, I suppose, to console himself. The bird had sung loudly enough before it had come away. In fact it had sung its head off while it was in the company of its brothers but it might mope and never sing again. It certainly seemed that way. It didn't get onto its perch that day. The next day, however, it perched although it sat dejectedly without gathering its flight feathers or flirting its tail. Sometimes its eyes closed and there was speculation that it might have caught a chill. I remember telling Grandmother that what was really needed was one of those goldies which Willie, the byre boy, caught with a handful of seed and a corn riddle. The goldie would soon have this strange, green and yellow bird singing but Willie couldn't catch goldies out of season. Goldfinches only came about the steading at harvest time to feed on the seeds of weeds in the old stackyard. When this kind of material was plentiful it took an expert to lure one under a riddle. No one took my suggestion seriously and it was generally accepted that the bird would never sing. The trauma of its long journey down from Glasgow had deprived it of its voice and it didn't even cheep. Father had some kind of bird tonic in a little bottle and added this elixir to the canary's drinking water, but it did no good. Grandfather suggested whisky. The tiny teaspoonful that was added to the water only seemed to depress the bird. Grandfather himself might get red-cheeked and sing when he had a wee dram in him, but canaries, it seemed, became more morose. Father and Mother departed for Glasgow without hearing the bird cheep. One of my aunts attended to its wants every day, blowing the husks from the seed container, giving it a little more seed and fresh water and 'cheep-cheeping' to encourage the creature to show it was still interested in living. It was a pity, Father had said, that conditions were primitive. You couldn't make the sound of running taps by working the handle of a pump or that might have done the trick. A kettle was left to sing on the range but still the canary didn't respond. Even my aunts, who were inordinately proud of their brother who worked on 'flying machines', privately expressed the opinion that the bird should have been kept where it belonged. It was a town bird. Everything brought up in the town had some quirk about it. Townspeople themselves were notoriously fastidious about all kinds of things. One day, my aunts said, shaking their heads, they would come down and find that poor bird lying on its back on the bottom of the cage and then maybe Willie would catch them a goldie to replace it. The bird, however, must have taken a turn for the better. At noon each day Grandfather, who would have all his other meals at a small round table on the other side of the kitchen, presided over his workmen while they took their dinner. He was the master and he would have no idiotic guffawing. He would insist that everyone sat up properly. No one put his head down to spoon soup from the rim of the bowl directly into his ever-open mouth! Nevertheless, there was always a buzz of conversation and everyone would speak at once. To tell the truth it was impossible to hear a person speak at times. Amid this clamour, one bright summer's day, Grandfather suddenly thumped the table. He would have silence and there was silence, or almost. In that hush the song of the bird was magical! It stood on its perch, its throat feathers ruffled, its head turning this way and that like an ecstatic starling singing in the morning sun. The song was a song without end and what an occasion that was! The men gazed up at the cage. Grandfather and Grandmother smiled happily. My aunts themselves twittered like singing birds in chorus. They would write and tell my father the bird had found its voice, without his tonic, without recourse to the whisky bottle that made Grandfather sing!

I listened to the canary because it was one of the first I had heard singing. The men went back to their work. Grandfather, after he had smoked his pipe, which didn't discourage that variegated canary one little bit, stomped off to supervise their labour. The bird, releasing something that had remained pent up for weeks, sang on and on.

Would it ever stop? I, too, went off out. My aunts and Grandmother got on with their chores of baking scones or scrubbing wooden chairs. The bird was wound up. It was still singing when I came back, as I always did, to beg for a hot scone, freshly buttered and covered with rhubarb or gooseberry jam. That sound soon became part of the other back-ground sounds of the kitchen. So long as there was enough light to sing by the bird would sing. Sometimes when the old gramophone was played it would perk up even more and give us one of its favourites by lamplight. My aunts began to consider covering the cage the way people did when a parrot became too talkative, but Grandmother said the bird was expressing happiness. That was something nobody should ever discourage either in a bird or a man! I don't think Grandfather took to the singing canary quite as much as the womenfolk. He became accustomed to the song. Once in a while, when the bird busied itself preening or stirring through its seed, he would look up and wonder why there was silence. The bird lived to be fourteen. I was on the verge of manhood when it died. It spent a whole lifetime singing, and I can hear it yet, a shrill and incessant song. Its world was wonderful. It was a bird of paradise. It seemed to love the smoky ceiling, the scent of burning wood and peat, and perhaps even Grandfather's acrid tobacco smoke. It didn't care whether anyone noticed it or not. Its purpose in life was to sing. As long as it lived it did that. Father was delighted. When he and Mother returned from time to time he would look at the bird and suggest he might give it a shampoo with a badger hair shaving-brush the way he shampooed his own birds, for the variegated one was beginning to look distinctly sooty. My aunts would have none of it. Wash the bird and it would catch a chill and die. It was healthy and happy. Its singing proved that. Willie, who overheard this conversation, chipped in with the thought that washing would weaken it. His father had never taken a bath but once. After that his back was no good and he couldn't lift a sack off the granary floor! Father, who would have performed the shampoo operation with all the skill of a canary-breeder, and dried the bird wrapped in a flannel before the fire, smoothing out its plumage with another little soft brush, or even 'polished' its feathers with a silk handkerchief, had to retreat. The bird remained unwashed all its life but was none the worse for that.

I remember, long after I had been taken to live with my parents and had moved down to Middlesex, coming back to the farm and hearing the bird singing in the kitchen even before I crossed the threshold. It was singing when my grandmother died. Unaware of the grief of the family, it sang in the kitchen when friends came to offer their condolences. It sang when I stood in line with Father and Grandfather and country people filed past the kitchen steps to shake our hands one after the other. It sang when the Minister conducted a short service preparatory to our setting out on that long, slow procession to the town and the cemetery on the hill. It was still singing on our return. Dear me, my aunts sobbed, how Grandmother had loved to hear the bird singing. No one had ever dared neglect it or Grandmother would have been angry. She would never have it 'happed' over to make it hold silence. She would be happy to know that, on this sad day, it was singing for her! It was all very sentimental and maudlin I am afraid but the bird was a member of the family. It was brought down when the cage was cleaned. Its seed and sand were renewed but one of the half dozen wild cats that came in for porridge and milk and to warm themselves in the hearth would have killed it, had it not been hoisted aloft again.

Father went on to bigger and better things, however. When we moved south he had dispensed with all his breeding cages and his stock of prize Border canaries, but he wasn't by any means cured. After a little while he went off and brought another canary, a singing bird which, when he came home or had a free day, he would talk to and train to hop from perch to perch, using his pencil like a conductor's baton. By chance a lady who lived nearby had also gone in for a canary. Mr and

Mrs Currer had become our close friends and the dilemma of Mrs Currer was that her canary didn't sing. Here we were again with a mute it seemed, but Father made a closer inspection of the songless bird and discovered that it was a hen. Canaries are bred in a particular way, a yellow cock mated to what is called a buff hen, and vice versa. I never really got to know why this is so but Mrs Currer's hen was a buff one. Our cock canary was a yellow. There and then the die was cast so far as Father was concerned. Off he went and brought materials to build a breeding cage, 'borrowing' our neighbour's bird and promising to produce a singer by breeding one. Mother had seen it all before. She was going to have none of it, but Father's plans must have had long standing. He had built a very solid shed in which he now proposed to breed canaries. The shed was well-lit, snug and draught-proof, but well-ventilated. All along one wall he would have flight cages. It was a tremendous project to provide a neighbour with a singing bird, but of course the provision of a single bird had never been Father's intention. He had become obsessed with a dream of surrounding himself with beautiful singing birds. He was quite fascinated to think of breeding mules and hybrids. It was no mere chance that a canary was a relative of the finch. In fact it must have been ordained by God that man should breed crosses, beautiful goldfinch, or greenfinch-canaries, canary-linnets and canary-bullfinches! Aviculturists know all the permutations of the business. Their world is a world apart, more fascinating than breeding livestock of any other kind. They find their experiments a continuing delight and, even although they occupy themselves with size and colour and variations in breeding mules and hybrids, they really love birds and this can't be said for a lot of dog-breeders.

Father was a particularly busy man. He worked long hours at the drawing board and the planning table. He often came home exhausted. His birds did a great deal to relieve the tension from working out how a particular aircraft component might be manufactured. Alas, he had little time for the chores involved in keeping, first a few pairs of birds, and then a score. He ceased to buy seed by the pound and bought it by the stone and then by the sack! The birds sang to deafen each other. There were pot nests and swan's down linings for them everywhere. Such a population explosion would have to have been seen to be believed. Hundreds of canaries went into the discard and were sold to dealers. The money from these transactions went to buy more highly-bred birds! Finally Father embarked on showing canaries, first as a novice of course, and then as a champion. Whenever there was a knock at the door, it seemed, another fancier was there with a bird in a cage! Mother complained bitterly, not only of the traffic but of the assorted characters who called. There are no class barriers in this particular world. Poor men and rich men love birds and enjoy breeding them. Father had many contacts, miners who bred canaries, aristocrats who had fine bird rooms and aviaries, all of them enthusiasts who hoped to make a name for themselves if not a fortune. Most canary-breeders make no money at all from their hobby. In those days they would only sell one bird to buy another. Father's country background had taught him something about the condition of birds and he believed in providing his with natural wild seed as well as the everyday canary seed. Wild seed, plantain and thistle, contained things that shop-bought and long stored seed lacked. It was to supply this seed that I, his juvenile dogsbody in the canary shed, was sent to gather wild seeds as well as groundsel and chickweed salad. I would spend quite a long time each morning in the shed, changing water, winnowing seed hoppers and so on, and sometimes thawing waterdishes before I went to school. I hated the chores, but I was given a penny or two pocket money for my labour and spent it in the school tuckshop. How I loved to be free to wander in the, at that time, open countryside surrounding the London suburb in which we lived. Here on the old pastures of farms that were still occupied but seemed unworked, I would gather thistle, teazle and plaintain rat-tails that were fat with large seed, superior to anything obtained in a so-called pet shop. I could also, in season, find a nest or two and indeed I found the nests of an extraordinary number of birds, finches, whitethroats, and a small bird I never saw or knew the proper name of, but the prince of bird's-nesters, with whom I struck an acquaintance, called it a 'nettle-creeper'. My wandering was far and wide. Once I remember I brought back the eggs of a chaffinch and, although my father lectured me about robbing the nest, he set the eggs under one of his canaries, and hatched a chaffinch brood. A year later we had chaffinch-canaries and canary-chaffinches. They were quite as handsome as the bullfinch-canary or the goldfinch-canary Father bred.

I was also involved, much against my will, in the business of showing canaries and made long journeys by tram or trolley bus to present Father's entries at a show. It was never the prize that mattered but the distinction of breeding the outstanding specimen. There was never going to be an end to it all it seemed. I was in my teens and still press-ganged as a bird-minder. The only relief I found was when I was sent to gather seed. I met one or two of the wild bird trappers who plied their trade in Middlesex and liked them no more than the Galloway bird-catcher. They were guilty men, always furtive and aware that the police or the 'cruelty-people' were on their trail when they got wind of what they were up to. The bird market in London was a thriving one and every sort of native singing bird could be bought at that time, over or under the counter, although today things are better regulated. Unscrupulous 'breeders' would show and sell cage-bird finches that had no time to get used to the cage and revealed their wild origin by baldness. A wild bird flies so often to the top of the cage in the first two or three days that its feathers are knocked out. On the other hand, given time, the wild bird settles, its feathers grow again. Only an expert, knowing the cage bird so well, can tell one from another.

Once again, it all had to end. Father was promoted and moved North to bigger and better things and I escaped those chores, at last. The hundreds of birds were sold and their cages dismantled. Father's career finally denied him the opportunity to dally with singing birds after that. I was exposed at an early age but the disease, so far as cage birds went, never took hold, I am happy to say.

14 A FINAL FLING

Father's retirement, as it nearly always does for someone whose life's work is at an end, posed a problem about where he would live. It wasn't just a matter of wanting to live in more pleasant surroundings than he had lived in when he commuted to Manchester, but of finding a place with enough room to go about without neighbours peering over the fence. He wanted a garden, with greenhouses and to keep bees and enlarge on things that had hitherto occupied a limited leisure. He finally found a place that pleased him and, because the property was near our house in North Wales, he telephoned to ask me to go and look at it. With the cottage went about four acres of ground, four green-houses, a potting shed and a long-established, large vinery. There was also an old orchard and a kitchen garden. Well, Father said, if he didn't cultivate the very large kitchen garden he might keep a few hens. Mother must have heard a bell ringing somewhere, but she said nothing. She knew how restless Father would be without something to occupy every hour of the day. The property would have been ideal for a young man full of enthusiasm to work the land. It was a place once kept by half a dozen gardeners. There was in fact, a hen-house which had once served as a piggery, and a wired-off hen-run at the far end of the kitchen garden. At first when they moved in, which they did after I had reported on all the features of the place and summed up the pros and cons of their doing so, Father resisted the urge to begin immediately keeping fowl, but soon he was putting up poles and making his first hen-run. It had netting reaching more than six feet from the ground. He thought this would keep out the fox, although I doubted that it would, for a fox can scramble over high netting, without difficulty. The fox didn't come, however. He stayed outside and lived somewhere on the top of the cliff. In the end old Charley was shot when Father co-operated with his neighbour, that farmer down below, but that is another story.

Mother wasn't too happy about the hens. She knew the scheme might be to keep a dozen but they would end up with a hundred, and she was right. Not only did the place swarm with hens but Father fell for ducks and geese before he was finished. What was intended to have been a delightful hobby became a tyranny of fowl-keeping, an inescapable chore morning and afternoon, day in and day out. At first Father would buy a bag of hen-food and bring it back in the boot of the car, but by the end of it all a lorry came once a month with a score of sacks. The point-of-lay pullets lived up to their pedigree and laid more eggs than Father and Mother could have eaten in a lifetime. The eggs were traded to the family grocer, although never at a profit. Father daren't produce accounts. His eggs weren't even paying the feed bill. He decided he would breed his own strain of Rhode Island-Anconas and White Leghorns, not to mention Light Sussex-Rhode Islands. He would trudge up to the far away hen-house on a bitterly cold and wet winter afternoon to stand and study his birds and come back down with new ideas. The summer house was up in the wood in those days. It seemed the ideal thing for conversion into a snug hen-house with a built-on laying compartment in which individual hens could be entrapped and their laying capacity recorded. The summer house was taken down and moved from the wood to the top of the kitchen garden. It was assembled on four concrete plinths, which, because of the slope below, facilitated the construction of a shed into which the birds could go in a downpour. The whole thing was built like a battleship, to last forever. The beauty of that space below the hen-house was that it could also serve as a duckhouse! Even geese could be accommodated there. Father laboured long over the construction of the hen-house and the shed beneath which was 'walled' with heavy slate slabs. There was nothing Mother could say to persuade Father he was wearing himself out in this final fling. He went to market and bought himself Khaki Campbell ducks and some longnecked Indian Runners. Emden and Toulouse geese followed. Suddenly it all looked like Old MacDonald's farm. Father, not content with two hen-houses and three hen-runs, had the dog kennel moved up from behind the potting shed to serve as another hen-house. I hasten to say that the kennel was an outsize one that had once housed an enormous St Bernard dog. In fact the former occupant of the kennel who had been taken to live some miles away, arrived on a walkabout one afternoon, hoping perhaps to reclaim his old kennel. I doubt whether his owners had been able to provide him with quite such a large shelter at their new premises. The converted kennel now accommodated at least two dozen Rhode Island hens in comfort after perches were installed and the door modified.

The Anconas were most handsome birds and the Rhode Island-Ancona crosses laid well. Father spent a lot of money on a pure white Leghorn cockerel, a showbench type of bird that looked magnificent. It was highly strung and delicate, however, and not used to the rough and tumble of a hen-run, even in the company of pure-bred Leghorn hens. It moped and died, much to Father's dismay. He had thought to breed more pure white Leghorns, considering the common Leghorn anybody's bird. He had always been for novelty and the challenge of such birds. When his flock numbered over sixty and he often had to fill the back of the car with egg crates he turned his attention to duck-rearing. There would be crossbreds here, too, he decided and at once he got down to producing a better Christmas goose than the common or garden birds obtainable in the market place. His would be the very finest Emden-Toulouse you ever saw! In the meantime, in the compounds of Father's private concentration camp, the collections of fowl cropped the very last blade of grass and paddled the earth into mud. The geese laid but once a year. The Khaki Campbell Ducks were great layers, however, and there was a problem in disposing of eggs not quite so popular as the brown egg from the best laying strain of hen. Father wasn't in the least daunted. A line had to be drawn between commercial enterprise and breeding bigger and better birds, and then there was another line to be drawn between experiment and research. What if a new strain of layer might be produced, not by a someone in an agricultural research department, but by an amateur? Father knew it would take years, but he never stopped to think how many years might lie ahead: he thought he would live forever. The cocks crowed every morning and somehow that guaranteed another day, and another. Between times he would hurry into the vinery to thin bunches of grapes he had no hope of selling, or into the old orchard to pick apples and pears he could hardly find room to store. Weeds grew and he hacked at them with a sickle and tore into them with a scythe, exhausting himself. He had always been a kind of human dynamo, a little man of light build, boundless energy and enthusiasm, but now he was wearing himself out. Mother became ill and he didn't know what to do about it all. He had never been able to bring himself to kill a cockerel for the pot. One day when I arrived I found Mother greatly agitated. Father had decided she might feel better with some roast chicken. He had steeled himself to sacrifice one of his prize birds but, alas, had bungled the killing. The cockerel, still alive, and kicking, was in a sack in the potting shed. Father had retreated to the lounge and sat with his head in his hands, distressed at his failure, and unable to finish what he had begun. I hastened to the potting shed and made an end of the wretched cockerel. Father had failed to wring its neck and then tried to kill it with a chopper! The whole thing had become a trauma. There was nothing I could say to console him. Incidentally, although the bird was cooked neither of them could eat it. Anyone who keeps birds for the table must take care never to allow himself to become involved with them, to give them names and look them in the eye, for then they cease to be of the generality of animals and become individuals. A farmer will tell you this. A pet lamb must be cast out. A pig with a personality must be sold to the butcher as quickly as possible. In every group of hens or ducks there will be at least one character, one bird that cocks its head and seems to have a higher intelligence than the average. Father's birds were all more than mere acquaintances. He knew them as a shepherd knows his sheep. That cockerel didn't need to crow thrice. Father had betrayed him. It was about this time that he began to lose heart. He was incapable of getting rid of his flock and he couldn't neglect them. He had enslaved himself and there was no way out, although he never mentioned how he felt.

For a time he brightened up when a gardener on the property down below invited him to come down and catch a strange bird that had suddenly appeared in the grounds. It seemed pheasant-like but wasn't a pheasant. It was bigger than a partridge and the colour of a woodcock. It was reluctant to fly but elusive in the undergrowth. Perhaps Father could trap it and add it to his flock? What they had come across turned out to be a corncrake. The bird had somehow lost the power to fly. Father telephoned me and set about catching it. Had a corncrake ever been kept in a pen? Would it survive? It was obviously a bird that might fall prey to a hunting cat or a fox. Father thought he might keep it long enough to restore it so that it could migrate in due course. The trouble was that a corncrake is a largely insectivorous bird with a liking for things like beetles, earwigs, grasshoppers, daddy-long-legs and small worms. Father's fowl had long since devoured even the larvae and eggs of most of those to be found in the kitchen garden. Nevertheless Father contrived to rig up a net in the undergrowth in which the seemingly half-tame corncrake was feeding. In due course, the bird, hurrying away as Father moved towards it, became enmeshed in the net and was taken. It 'died' in his hand as soon as he picked it out of the net, but this is something a corncrake will do when captured and it recovered. It was brought up to the cottage and Father spent an afternoon with a jam jar catching grasshoppers which he put into the box in which he had housed the 'grass quaill' as it used to be called. The run where the Anconas were kept happened to be fenced with small-mesh netting. It seemed to be a suitable place in which to keep the corncrake during its convalescence. Although the corncrake ignored the grasshopper feast put before it, it ran down to take shelter under some brushwood Father had put in the run to give it cover. It was there the following day but Father couldn't be sure the hens hadn't harried it and devoured the beetles and small worms he had dropped into the brushwood. I was excited to hear of the crake's survival. I knew the bird from boyhood when I had found its nest in the long grass. It was years since I had seen one and I hadn't heard its call for a long time. Father hoped that in a week or two this shy bird of the long grass would take off and fly out, fully recovered from whatever it was that had reduced it to skulking in the undergrowth, but this wasn't to be. One afternoon, just before I arrived at the cottage, the crake came uphill. Perhaps it was looking for something more to its taste than the limited sorts of insect Father was able to provide. Suddenly it was caught in the open by those beady-eyed hens who rushed at it and pecked it to death. Father blamed himself for not keeping the bird in isolation. I turned it over in my hand. It was emaciated. It had never been going to fly out. It was, in fact, the last corncrake I saw or heard in Wales, though later on I saw scores in the far West of Ireland and listened to them calling all through a summer night as they did in my childhood.

Something of the sort happened when I brought a young mallard to the cottage that summer. I was fishing a mountain lake when, crossing a boggy patch of ground, I came upon a mallard duck that had fallen prey to a fox minutes before my arrival. The duck lay, and beheaded, in shallow water. There were fox tracks on the otherwise smooth peat bank round the waterhole. I looked about for ducklings. It seemed to me that the duck hadn't been taken unawares but had played that old game of feigning injury to lure the fox from her brood, yet the fox had somehow managed to get her. The ducklings had made their escape but would perish without their mother. I searched diligently and managed to find one which I picked up and popped into my fishing creel along with some grass. The duckling still had its mahogany dapples. I thought Father might be able to do something with it and took it to the cottage on my way home. Once again Father exerted himself to succour the wild bird and gave it food with a pair of tweezers. It proved more ready to feed than the crake. For a while it seemed to be going to make it, but when he released it in the run it looked too much like a scurrying rat. The hens rushed at it and killed it. Father had forgotten his lesson. He was grieved to think that birds were as ruthless with one another as human beings. I remembered him urging me to shoot a sparrowhawk when he had come upon it clutching a lovely little long-tailed tit that was nesting in a gorsebush behind the long green-house. There was always something naïve and childlike in the way he looked at the animal kingdom and birds in particular. He wouldn't seem to see that a hawk is a hawk, just as a fox is a fox, and both are parts of the whole system.

Mother died in the autumn of that year. Father's great flock of birds kept him at his daily labour. His bees had never really done well after being transported from Cheshire. He neglected them now, but the hens, ducks and geese clamoured for his attention and had to be fed, watered and locked up every night. Father's foot was nailed to the ground. He couldn't be away for long because he had to get back to feed the birds or lock them up. He had hen-houses to clean and eggs to gather, even though it was all getting beyond him. Finally he was taken ill and was rushed to hospital for an immediate operation. I had to take over. It was spring. His birds, lacking the exercise they might have had if the hard ground had been turned over so that they could scrape and scratch, had gone in for a go-slow. Egg production had dwindled. Every day when I visited Father in hospital the first thing he would ask was how were his birds, and I would give an account of my labour. We had gone to stay at the cottage to look after everything now, and I spent a lot of my time getting the Rhode Island-Anconas and Light Sussex to lay. I provided them with fresh greenstuff. I broke my back digging up runs. The ducks and geese looked much better for the attention I gave them and the grass I provided by a scything session. The hens started to lay as never before and exceeded their norm. Lying in hospital for seventeen weeks, Father issued fresh instructions every day and made new plans. I was glad when at last he was discharged for I had never worked so hard in all my life.

There was to be no winding down. Not one hen, cockerel, duck, drake, goose or gander would be parted with! Father soldiered on. His steps were heavier. The birds were cared for, but they had gone back to their old ways and laid half as many eggs as they used to, because, of course, they were growing older and Father hadn't been there to set hens on eggs to produce more point-of-lay pullets. The food bill was beyond all reason. Once again Father became ill. This time his symptoms were more ominous. A physician diagnosed a secondary cancer but he was wrong. The cancer was not a secondary one but another one altogether.

Exactly one year after he had first gone into hospital Father went back again – for two weeks, at the end of which he died. For a good part of his life he had been obsessed with cage birds and fowl of one sort and another. I was left to do what he had not been able to bring himself to do, to dispose of the livestock, tidy up the compounds and finally dismantle them. I had mixed feelings about it. Father's ghost haunted me, walking up or down from the kitchen garden and his hen-houses. I advertised the birds and sold them in batches. The gardener who had brought him news of the corncrake came up to buy 'them ducks of your Dad's'. I gave them to him and the geese as well. An essentially practical and quite unsentimental being, the gardener had no hesitation in putting the ducks to the sword. I thought about the way they would follow the old man about, quacking happily and pestering him for just another handful of meal, and the way the geese would sometimes tweak at his coat for titbits.

I finally took down the concentration camp, dismantled the laying compartment bolted onto the summer house and restored the house to its former purpose after scraping and disinfecting it and giving it a coat of creosote. The silence in the kitchen garden was unnatural. Grass began to grow where the hens had made the ground bare and I planned to plough when we moved in, for that is what we had decided to do after the business of Father's estate was settled. The executors weren't too pleased at my selling the livestock for a paltry sum and I didn't tell them I had given the ducks and geese away. We couldn't have eaten any of them. I made up my mind never to keep hens. I hoped I would never fall into that trap and tie myself down with fowl, trudging up and down to feed and lock up hens on a cold winter's day. There would be no cock crow at dawn. This was an abandoned, romantic dream. A man must learn from his father's mistakes and avoid the pitfalls his father might have fallen into. These were my sentiments when we came to live at the cottage. I had enough to do getting greenhouses mended, vines pruned and cured of mildew, the old trees in the orchard sprayed and a thousand other chores done. My plan was to grow food for the family. Poultry-keeping was not for me, nor was beekeeping. The bees had died when Father died. As I had done with the hen-houses and the netted runs, I wheeled the hives away and made a tidy pile of them. My garden would be a vegetable garden. I wasn't going to run a smallholding. I little thought that in a few years I would be in the same trap as Father and keeping an even greater variety of birds.

15 HAWKS IN MY HANDS

Tracing exactly how I came to keep so many different fowl, I think it all began when the elder of my two sons, who was then a schoolboy, came home with a little owl. The bird wasn't properly fledged and it had that fascinating beauty of all immature raptors, a kind of hairy fluffiness on a reptilian framework, bright eyes and a wicked looking beak that still had to grow a bit, like the rest of its dumpy body. Owlets have this, so do the young of the kestrel, the larger falcons and, to a slightly lesser degree, the hawks, whose beaks are more perfectly designed for delicate work, like taking the skull of its victim apart with no need of the surgeon's trepanning tool! It seemed that the small owl had been found under a tree though little owls usually nest in holes in the ground. A friend of mine always insisted on calling them burrow owls, because they inhabited the maternity homes of wild rabbits, that always go out into the open field to have their litters. Whatever the cause of its being found in the open, the little owl couldn't be left to perish of cold and want of food, and so it was installed in our renovated hut that had been a hen-house. Thoughts of using the hut for its original purpose of a summer house were put aside. The small owl became its tenant although it was like keeping a mouse in a hay barn. I saw no harm in raising and rehabilitating the owl. It would provide a natural history lesson for the boys. I was being trapped, although I didn't realise what was happening, and the owl would lead to hawks and falconry, to keeping quail, gamebirds, golden pheasants, bantams, ducks of all kinds, including an enormous flock of muscovies, and even fighting cocks that would never wear metal spurs. For the time being the owl kept our elder boy busy, busy neglecting his studies, day-dreaming about the little comedian of an owlet that skulked in the darkest corner of the shed and came out timidly like a church mouse after it had listened to the silence. Andrew had no thought of the O levels and A levels he would need. He thought about insects, grasshoppers he would catch and feed into the hungry maw of the fledgling, beetles he might find here or there, or worms he would have to dig and cut up to keep the little owl from starving. As the bird grew it became more and more of a character. It would fly to perch on its keeper's shoulder and nestle against his head. It would squeak and bob and weave like a boxer avoiding blows, and keep its solemn eyes fixed on whoever seemed to be confronting it. Its flights soon extended to the full length of the hut and it began to wait for the door to be opened so that it could fly to its keeper. It looked at the world outside through the windows but it was in no condition to fly free or fend for itself. Little owls came to populate most of the country from Holland and for a long time were called Dutch owls. They are predatory but the main purpose of their hunting is to leave immediate prey to decompose so that it can be turned over in due course and the burying beetles, that gather to inter the corpse, devoured. The little owl's work is done in daylight and it is often seen perching on posts or pastureland trees in sunlight because this is its habit. It flies with a moth-like flight but always seems to be slightly top-heavy. It is quite the most fascinating of the owl species not just because of its size but its 'undertaking' habits. It is also a beautifully-marked little bird about the size of a blackbird or a smallish jackdaw. We got to know the little owl while Andrew whiled away his days looking after it. Everyone in the family became involved with 'Hibou' and then, when he was looking at his best and in the sheen of perfect condition, the comic little fellow died. We had lost a member of the family! For more than a week we were in mourning. No one mentioned 'Hibou'. He had been buried in a secret place but his grave marked with an enormous cross lay in the long grass. I didn't notice the grave for ten years and finally came upon it when I was cutting grass and brushwood. No more pets, we said. Susy, the Cairn, would be enough, but I reckoned without those pigeon-fanciers who had lofts on the allotments on the way into town. Their flighting birds drew Andrew like a magnet. Soon he was coming home late, not because he was in detention, which he might have been for his day-dreaming, but because he hung about the lofts. Pigeon-fanciers are always keen to encourage a youngster who shows interest in their hobby. Soon they were teaching Andrew how to pick up and handle a bird, spreading its wing across the ball of the thumb, how to put a ring on its leg or spot a change in its condition by studying its eye. Andrew should have been inoculated against pigeons, but instead he went down to the lofts and caught the disease. I didn't know it at the time, but he also passed it on to his younger brother! This wasn't the same strain of pigeonitis I had had from my father, who had simply loved to keep homers. This was the racing fancy with birds of a blood line, birds exercised like race-horses and always entered for novice events before they qualified for bigger prizes. It was inevitable that Andrew, with a present of a pair of good birds from one of the fanciers, would come home and suggest the old hen-house-cum-piggery at the far end of the kitchen garden might be converted into a pigeon loft, a loft with shelf perches and laying compartments, feeders and drinkers, and of course, a trap. A trap allows the birds to be released for morning flight but when they return afterwards they remain until their owners decide to release them again. I simply had to give in and allow the old hen-house to be converted into a loft and there had to be a trap, which I made for it. Trees were pruned to let the birds see the loft from afar and also give them a clear fly-in or flight path. The outer edge of the roof also needed to be fenced to prevent birds perching before entering the trap. (This is part of the racing pigeon keeper's guile. The bird must be trapped as soon as possible so that its ring can be taken off and 'processed' by the clock. At the start of every race clocks are gathered up, set and sealed and returned to their owners. They record time on a print-out. The ring recovered from the bird is put into the clock without delay for minutes are sometimes critical.)

The whole thing was bound to grow. The first two birds produced a pigeon pair, and then a second pair. New and better birds were found to breed better stock *ad infinitum*. I provided the money for corn, which had to be bought by the half hundredweight through the club. It delighted me to see a flight of pigeons speeding over the garden and climbing into the morning sky. I toyed with an old dream of my own to keep tumblers and fantails in a dovecote and perhaps pouters, even more exotic pigeons. Tumblers, I told myself, stay within sight of the loft and climb and tumble all day. They are sometimes called the birds of the longest day for on this day of the year their owners clock them out of the loft and hope that they will stay aloft all day. The fancier sits and watches along with a judge who endorses the record for the competition. Andrew managed to add a pair of tumblers to his collection of trim, sleek racing birds. The tumblers rose into the morning sunlight and did their epileptic falling at least twice before they 'homed' to the place they had come from. That was the end of it. I never did build a dovecote or get those little white fantails. The first flush of racing pigeons diminished without Andrew winning a prize in a race but he reared and raised many lovely racing pigeons. In the end he somehow became convinced that he must pay more attention to his schoolwork. It was a year or two before his brother Ian set it all up again. In the meantime an equally dangerous virus had got into my blood. I took up hawking.

I must say at the outset that an account of my involvement with hawks and falcons will show that I was always more interested in the birds than the so-called sport of falconry. I was not in the true mould of hawker or falconer. I saw the business of hunting hawks as something like keeping ferrets to get rabbits. Many cruel things used to be done to keep a ferret working. I have known an old countryman put a stitch in the poor creature's lips to prevent it drawing blood and lying to gorge on a rabbit it should have bolted. I have seen a ferret that had had its fangs snapped off with the same purpose in mind, and I saw one shot for continually refusing to go below and stay there. I never did like to see a falcon wearing a hood, however traditional this skilfully made piece of leather headgear may be. I never liked the mad battle of wills that takes place between a man and a goshawk, or the starvation tactic employed to bring a bird to hunting sharpness. A good hawk is a hungry hawk but the delicate balance between hunger and starvation is not something a novice can learn without making his bird suffer. All this apart, I was never convinced that all falconers have a genuine feeling for birds. Many seem to regard the hawk as a tool, a creature to be bent to the will. In this process the unfortunate creature is tied to a block for most of its life and brought up short every time it flies off the fist. I have often watched the tethered hawk and the way it looks into space. I became convinced in the end that the proper place for a noble falcon is the wild crag, and for the hawk, the tree from which it sweeps in pursuit of its chosen prey, once perhaps every two days or so, not to order, and not for the reward of a cube of raw meat. It should stand with its talons in its victim and feather it, feather by feather, and enjoy those intervals of looking about with the wind ruffling its plumage.

Be all this as it may, I fell among falconers as keen to explain how hawks are manned and flown as the pigeon-fanciers were to impart their secrets. All initiations seem to insist upon the humiliation of the candidate by impressing upon him his unfitness for what he has asked to be admitted to and his ignorance and lack of skill in the art. I was told I couldn't really expect to manage a falcon or a goshawk and almost became convinced that what I should have got myself was a stuffed bird and an old motoring gauntlet! I walked a few paces behind the experts, listened to their technical jargon and watched the way they flew their birds. The goshawk, manned or unmanned, seemed to be insane, as erratic as a hashish-drugged Arab, as unmanageable as a cornered wildcat. The baleful eye matched a beak that could whip out its owner's eye as efficiently as it split a pigeon's breast. It would sometimes fall as though in a fit, twirling at the end of the leash, its inverted head looking even more wicked than when right way up. The minute it was restored to the fist it would flap off and sometimes beat its master with its wings until he ducked out of the way or was almost blinded. I agreed with them when they said, I would have to graduate to a goshawk. To get myself one might be to end up in a madhouse, bearing in mind that needed to be a *wild* bird trained to *my* fist. The manning business might take me round the clock and continue for many days until my hawk accepted me and learned it would find food nowhere but in my hand. It would probably starve rather than do it my way. It might become so weak that it would die if I made a mess of things. It all seemed much too cruel for me. Well then, they said, the falcon is easier but more expensive but a novice may ruin a falcon and make it useless for hunting. He needs to know what he wants and have a special feeling for hawk or falcon. The ideal thing would be for me to learn how to handle a docile raptor like a buzzard, not a hunter's bird at all, but a scavenger: a buzzard sails about and takes a worm or a beetle as well as a rat, a vole or an occasional rabbit. It can't really be 'flown' at anything. I didn't care very much for this. I watched a red-tailed hawk (which is an American buzzard less inclined to scavange than our native species) fly after a hare and bring it down. It did so in a peculiarly leisurely way and without the dash of the goshawk or the dramatic swoop of the peregrine. Bonelli's eagle wafted along, rowing itself through the air, going just as fast as the goshawk without appearing to have its speed, but when it struck it hooded over its prey like a vulture. There seemed nothing noble about it. Before I started I knew I wasn't going to be much of a falconer: I wasn't prepared to serve the required apprenticeship. I wouldn't swim on one leg in the shallow end. I couldn't go in at the deep end. It was at this stage that a friend came along with a sickly hen sparrowhawk. I fell in love with that fierce little hawk in fawn, white-flecked tweed trousers, for the feathered legs of the female sparrowhawk always look like trousers. The beauty of the sparrowhawk is its yellowness of eye, bill and foot. The eye holds the key to all its behaviour for, unlike the dark eye of the falcon which blends with a dark iris, the yellow iride of the sparrow-hawk (and the goshawk) shows the size of the pupil as the bird surveys its surroundings. If the pupil becomes small and the bird is looking down a diminishing tunnel, a cone of vision that might be comparable with a camera lens as the diameter of the iris is varied. Watching this, a man with a hawk on his wrist can tell what is about to happen and occasionally may see what it is that is exciting his bird. Having been given a small hawk I knew it at once for a much more lively, more spirited creature, as a small version of the gos, than any of the falcons although my small bird was spared the sheer insanity and bloody-mindedness of the cook's hawk. I installed my invalid on a screen perch in the summer house. A hawk perched on a screen may tumble off in frustration but it always claws its way back up to the perch, using the screen before it spins round and round, and dies at the end of a twisted leash and plaited jesses. I fashioned a bow perch for the bird and searched for the right items of food so that its condition might be improved while its wings were recovering and it was being exercised on a long line. I taught myself the rudiments of hawk management while this was going on. I also had an opportunity to study the bird at close hand and learn its nature. A hawk may seem to have about as much brain as a lizard. It is apparently motivated by the need to eat and to fly free. Its eye holds the key. Only after keeping a hawk for months and spending days on end in its company does one learn its character. Some people hold that a hawk is never tamed and never accepts man. There are some animals, the wildcat and polecat among them, that are so wild, so fierce and highly-strung that they are untameable, but if a goshawk runs these a close second, the sparrowhawk *can* be tamed, not by starvation but by gentle handling, by patience and a calm approach. It is a most sensitive creature and having won its trust is in itself an accolade. The man who gets there learns to love the bird through long involvement with it. Alas for my first encounter with a hawk I persuaded to trust me, I foolishly left it to feast on the liver of a hare. The hare had been feeding where pesticides had been used on the pasture. Poison killed my bird before I was able to release it, as, despite my love for it, I was morally bound to do. I don't think I mourned the death of a relative more than the death of that slender, beautiful female sparrowhawk when I found it, lying on the grass in the sun, its feet clutching at something that wasn't there, its beak open and its lovely yellow eyes closed for good.

The friend who had left the bird in my care to be rehabilitated was inclined to laugh at sentimentality. To restore my spirits he insisted on my doing the same for another hawk someone had brought in, but I had had enough for the time being. I said I wasn't the right sort of person. I wasn't cut out to keep hawks let alone set myself up as a falconer. What a man sees depends upon where he stands or stations himself! But another visit from my friend persuaded me to perform a similar service again. This time the bird was the victim of a collision with telegraph wires. It was an even smaller sparrowhawk. A male weighing no more than three-and-a-half ounces. The male sparrowhawk has an even more delicate balance between condition and lack of condition, life and death. An overfed one becomes lethargic and then ill. A underfed one loses its strength and falls from its perch. Half an ounce may be the limit, and it needs to be put on the scales every day. It must be fed just the right kind of thing to ensure proper nourishment. Pelleting every two days or so makes it disgorge things like fur and bones which have aided digestion. The bird always limes its waste by cocking its tail. Lack of pellets indicates that digestion is being impaired. A green rather than a white excrement means trouble. In order that the bird can get enough calcium it has to be fed things like small birds and mice. It won't do simply on a diet of shredded steak or minced beef. For things to be perfect, it must perch in the sun, be brought in from the rain (in case it contracts a chill) and be given a dish of water to take a bath although it doesn't need to drink water as most birds must.

My small sparrowhawk came through a long winter. That in itself was an achievement. Most old hawkers consider that a male sparrow-hawk, which, in any case, can't be used except to hunt small birds, needs to be returned to the wild before the end of autumn for it won't come through winter on a perch. My bird did, and it was in beautiful condition. I had established a relationship with a small hawk and it would fly to me without being called. One day in the garden I watched its excitement over a blackbird picking on the ground at the bottom of the slope. When the blackbird took wing I let the little hawk go. He killed the blackbird before it reached the far hedge. I came to the conclusion that he didn't need what hawkers call hacking back for he hadn't forgotten what it was about! I cut the small jesses off his legs. He flew away. It was hard to admit he had gone without showing the slightest inclination to return, but he belonged in the wild. I had no right to keep him tied to my hand.

My final 'affair' was with the genuine falcon, a lanner, which, like the lagger, is a foreign species, and a particularly handsome bird, smaller in size than a peregrine and more docile. I kept this bird for a while, flew it free once or twice, brought it through a throat infestation called frounce caused by a parasite that generally makes an end of a hawk, and finally sold it for the price I gave for it, winding the whole thing up and hanging up my falconer's glove for good. I have never regretted the time I spent studying falcons and falconers but the birds were much more worthwhile as a subject than some of the people who flew them.

16 THE COCK CROW

Looking back I can see now it was inevitable that I followed in my father's footsteps. I had a mental picture of myself keeping fowl. A dream came from my subconscious. It all began in a small way, I suppose, with Japanese quail, which I didn't keep because I had a gourmet's taste for this small bird but because I had a vision of myself stocking fields with quail. All the pastures of Anglesey might one day have these miniature, feathered helicopters whirring out of the long grass before a moving machine or forager got to them. Anglesey had, here and there, the migrant European quail about it still. Quail had also thriven, once upon a time when it was all a peaceful, corncrake's world, in the Galloway of long ago. My dream was lovely. In it I released my little quail but in fact when I did they retreated before the frost and never came back. Quail were only a small part of my dream, however. I heard the cock crow and I was a child in a world where, on a bright summer's day as rooks descended on the turnip hills, cocks crowed to one another across acres of arable land and green pastures. The cock crow was the very morning of my life in golden sunlight; with it went the drone of bees gathering nectar and swallows flitting in and out of cart shed and byre. I meant to have that cock crow back and would keep a jaunty little bantam cockerel to herald the morning and please me crowing all day long. It was a quite sentimental dream, but most of my dreams are. I didn't think of the bitterly cold mornings when I would have to thaw out the drinkers or the dreary winter afternoons with the log fire making me sleepy while I had to tear myself away from it to shut up the birds. My dream was to have the kind of bantams the blacksmith kept when I was a boy, those happy little birds that took dustbaths in his garden and ran for the shelter of the bushes when rain threatened. I could hear their crowing echoing in the great cathedral of the wood beyond the smithy. That too, I would hear in my own wood beyond the cottage, and so, when I had done with hawks and put them from me once and for all, I found my half-dozen bantams. My first cockerel was a sturdy blue-black Rosecomb, perfect in every detail from head to tail. He was accompanied by half a dozen hens, one of which was cream-coloured and patterned with 'beech leaves', and another, a 'partridge', looked like the native English partridge. I would have had a tall-in-the-leg, fierce-looking Indian Game had one been to hand, for as a boy I had been fascinated by Indian Gamecocks my Grandfather kept. My small flock multiplied. I bred more. I found new birds to avoid inbreeding. In a year I had four cockerels crowing. The headcount of cockerels later went to fifteen! What had been a fancy became an obsession. The thing was in my blood, a congenital weakness. In a similar way, in spite of an early determination to get rid of my father's beehives, I came to keep bees and have, in the end, even more colonies than he had once had.

Along with the bantams there would be ducks, Aylesbury, Khaki Campbell, one or two crossbreds resulting from a hatch of duck eggs I brought back from the new owners of the farm where I had spent my childhood, and no less than forty-eight muscovies! The only water on the place was an old bath which I set in the ground but had to fill with earth because my bantams insisted on trying to swim with the ducks. As some people may know even muscovies can get along well without a pond. Mine laid eggs everywhere, vying with lay-away bantam hens who would emerge from the undergrowth every three weeks or so with chicks trailing behind them. The blackboard on which I had kept a record of the changes in weight of my hawk, became a tallyboard for my flock: 12 brown hens, 72 bantams, 48 muscovies, 7 misc ducks, 12–14 cockerels and a pair of golden pheasants! Noah would never have taken half that number into his ark. The birds hurried towards me when I went to feed them and the cocks never stopped crowing. It was difficult to count them at any time and impossible when there was a mêlée round the hut as I scattered pellets and corn and tried to forget the food bill my self indulgence was running up. It had to come to an end, of course. I couldn't let it go on the way it was going. The ducks had to be found new homes. I gave muscovies to anyone who would take them. I kept brown hens that laid brown eggs but I dithered over a cull of cockerels because I was so fond of each and every one of them. There is no bird I love so much as a cocky bantam, and my bright-eyed little cockerels looked me in the eye so steadily that I began to believe they were aware they had a hold over me. One day when I was up at the depot getting another twelve bags of food and writing a cheque for it someone asked me if I was getting a good return in eggs. It was the autumn of the year. Bantams go off the lay, as indeed other domestic fowl do, once a year. It is said bantams don't lay while there are blackberries for the picking. Mine weren't laying. Only the old brown hens, from the laying strain, were keeping their end up, although some were only laying on alternate days, for even a laying hen comes to the end of her useful life, but I thought about those cockerels. The cock crows but he can't lay eggs, my grandmother told me when I was five years of age. I wasn't old enough to realise the significance of what dear old granny said. Perhaps she was a feminist of some kind. Perhaps she was simply stating a fact of life. The following day, instead of opening the hen-house door, I went in with two sacks and collared ten bantams which I conveyed down to the hut. There, steeling myself, I drew their necks. It was an outrageous thing to have done. I told myself it was over. It shamed me, when, digging a trench, I buried the birds the same morning. I didn't want to be with myself. I went indoors and took a large glass of whisky. It wasn't ten o'clcok. A fine start to the day, whichever way you might choose to look at it! I noticed long intervals in the cock crow that day. Four cockerels couldn't possibly crow like fourteen.

Whatever number of hens may accept a mature cockerel as their lord and master, nature seems to see to it that a hatch of eggs laid by bantams results in a fifty-fifty balance of male and female. To avoid this, eggs have to be sexed, something beyond any capability. Inevitably there were bound to be more young cockerels to be culled, I told myself. At this stage I went off to visit a friend in the Staffordshire area, and there, as free as my own half-wild flock of birds, I admired Duckwing Game. Nothing would please my friend but I should accept a trio, two wheaten hens and a fine young cockerel! There was more to this than the acquisition of three birds of pure strain. The cock, like the one in *Will Waterproof's Lament*, was of a finer egg and upon a finer dunghill trod. If he didn't rake golden barley and was fed a more balanced diet, he crowed late and early. He was a fighting cock, who, although he hadn't been matched in battle, came, like the bulls of Spain, from generations of fighters. His blood was not just red, but full of fire. He was a descendant of survivors of cockfighting all the way back to John Ardsoif, who drew up the rules for the main at St James's, Westminster. I actually had these rules hanging in my house and John Ardsoif's seal on them.

I was told to watch out when I put this fighting bird down for his hackles would go up and he would challenge any other cockerel at hand. He would destroy his rivals for he looked at the world through a haze of blood. I must say he was the handsomest cockerel I had ever had. His tail hung so gracefully. The white on his wings contrasted with the blue that gives this particular breed the name of Duckwing. He held his head high. He was a picture-book bird. I brought him home in a basket along with two wheaten hens and penned him that night in darkness. I heard him crow in the morning. When I went up I saw the impatient way he paced the wire. He was in new surroundings where he could hear other cocks crowing. He was ready to prove himself cock of the walk. I tried to prevent this at all costs, but I reckoned without four foolish birds already in the little orchard. They came to look at the prisoner and give him a dab or two to let him know what he could expect when he was out among them. Fools that they were they didn't recognise a killer. They saw him as a newcomer with a high opinion of himself but the newcomer was ferocious and fearless. He nailed three of the four through one-inch mesh, cutting their dangling combs and wattles and leaving them bloody, and, when the blood dried, black-faced. The fourth bird stayed in the background and avoided injury.

I had been advised to dub the Duckwing which meant trimming the comb and wattles with a pair of scissors. If this is done with care while the bird is young it is painless and there is very little blood. Dubbing, it is said, increases the bird's virility and reduces damage a rival may inflict by seizing wattles or comb to drag his victim about. I was nervous of performing the operation but it went off well. In a couple of days the Duckwing looked rather like a fighting cock shorn for the cockpit. I hasten to say I hold no brief for the barbarity of cock fighting, which, in spite of severe penalties, still goes on in this country. Like the bullfight it is a thing that degrades man. I didn't want my birds to fight one another. I wanted them to live in peace and harmony on the green grass of the orchard. Alas, it couldn't be that way. One morning when I was scattering food for the hens in the pen the aggressive Duckwing slipped out. I hadn't fastened the door properly. I didn't miss him until I saw a feather or two on the grass above the apple trees, and a drop of blood like a ruby in the dew. By this time my Creve Coeur cockerel was dead, his legs in the air, his wings twitching. Every now and then his body gave a convulsive jerk as though it was trying to throw itself back onto its legs, but the bird's eyes were closed. One stroke of the Duckwing's beak had pierced its skull like a blow from a pickaxe. The Hamburg had flown over the wall and cackled nervously out there in the tangle of briar and blackthorn. He probably escaped death by a matter of a minute or two. The Rosecomb was deep among the thorns of an old gooseberry bush. A little mongrel cockerel, who really should have been culled, had sensed danger and dived into the hedge at the bottom of the slope. The Duckwing crowed. There wasn't a mark on him. His blood was up and he quivered. I threw a stick at him but he sidestepped it like a boxer. He wasn't in the least daunted. I ran towards him and he ran, but he didn't scuttle. There was dignity about the way he avoided me. For a minute I wondered if I should put him down. De-beaking an alternative, perhaps, is a cruel business and I would still have to cut his spurs. There was nothing for it but to keep him securely penned. I did this making up my mind to reduce it all to one cockerel, which would allow the Duckwing his freedom. I made an end of the Rosecomb. His fine hackles were useful for fly-tying. The Hamburg didn't come back over the wall. I think a fox had a lying out place in the bushes and took the opportunity of getting himself a hot dinner. It grieved me. Both the pencilled Hamburg and Creve Coeur were pure-bred and very good birds. The Rosecomb too, was quite a specimen. I chased that fourth bird, the mongrel, for several days. He eluded me and roosted out, flying up every night like a jungle fowl and keeping out of the way whenever I visited the birds. Sometimes a cockerel seems to know he has been marked down. He reads something in his keeper's eye and knows he is for it! That lightweight kept well out of my way. I released the Duckwing. He never managed to catch the wild one. Occasionally the resourceful and wary little cockerel managed to persuade a couple of hens to keep him company in the wood, away from the Duckwing's territory. Things went on like this. In due course the Duckwing put his stamp on the flock. Young Duckwing cockerels appeared in the new generation but they began fighting one another once they were fledged. They fought for hours on end, stabbing, raising their hackles, posturing and sometimes throwing up their legs, trying to strike an opponent with both spurs at once. It was comic at first but then, as they grew older, there began to be fatalities.

I suppose the fifty-fifty sex balance has some kind of ecological factor governing it. If, in the wild, young cockerels battle and some die, in the end there will be one dominant bird, a survivor who will be responsible for more of his particular strain. I couldn't let this kind of thing happen, however; I didn't keep birds to watch them kill one another. I had to intervene again and cull the young cocks, leaving two to grow up alongside the mature Duckwing. One day, of course, they might offer battle to their father. One might die and the other run away to fight again another day and perhaps triumph. On the other hand, two or three generations would certainly produce a bird that would bring that original fighting cock low. One plays at being God breeding birds, but even this kind of exercise is subject to an immutable law. I solved the problem by parting with the original Duckwing cock and allowed one of his offspring to take over. Sad to relate, the old fellow contracted liver disease. He was brought back to me and thrived for a while until unforeseen disaster laid him low. The wild, roosting-out cockerel who had avoided a fatal encounter caught the Duckwing unawares one morning it seemed, for there he was, lying low on the wet grass when I went up to the little orchard, the great warrior apparently slain! I picked him up and was relieved to find I was mistaken. He wasn't quite dead, but he was cold and covered with blood. One eye had been taken out and the other was damaged. Full of compassion for him, I carried him to the hut and bathed his head, treated his eyes with diluted TCP and put him in a box in a nest of fresh hay. He didn't look as though he could make it, but he did. I put him back in the pen but he could barely see his food when it was put down for him. I hand-fed him and tended him for days until he began to feed properly. In the meantime I trapped the wild cockerel who had blinded the Duckwing and drew his neck. The surviving cockerel in the flock now was a Duckwing-Silkie cross and he became cock of the walk. He had those hair-like feathers of a Silkie and the Silkie's dark liver comb, but he had Duckwing wings and was a very unusual, handsome bird.

There was no other name for the Duckwing now but Blind Pugh, for it was obvious that he was blind. He would walk into me at times and collide with stones and boulders. He didn't look for a fight and reminded me of an old prize-fighter. My affection for him grew. I felt guilty that I hadn't trapped the wild cockerel long ago. When the Duckwing was in full health the lightweight bird couldn't have laid a spur on him, but he had caught the old fellow on a slope and fought him downhill. The Duckwing's eye had been put out in the first minute or two. It was all very very sad. Destroying the bird that had blinded the Duckwing was something I did out of a sense of guilt but Blind Pugh was there to remind me of my folly. The people to whom I had given him came back and shook their heads sadly. Perhaps the vet might do something to restore the sight of that one eye. A vet was consulted but he was adamant. The Duckwing simply had to be put down. No, it wasn't because he was blind. He was wasting away. Liver infection was going to kill him quite soon. He mustn't be allowed to suffer any longer. I grieved all the more. By now the Silkie-Duckwing was putting his mark on the flock. Permutations of Partridge, Wyandote, Araucana, Silkie, and of course, Duckwing Game resulted in a highly unsuual flock of birds. The Araucanas lay blue eggs and the pure-bred strain had a crow-like head. People who breed bantams are careful to avoid mixing strains like this because it leads nowhere but keeping bantams is one thing, breeding them quite another. Breeding a pure strain is exacting and scientific business. I had often thought of penning trios to breed perfect birds, but the work involved, with all the other things I needed to do, was too much to contemplate.

Not long after the death of Blind Pugh a decision had to be taken about the entire flock for we found ourselves having to move to a part of the world where the fox holds sway and will burrow and bite his way into pens if he finds no food outside. Keeping bantams so far as I am concerned is at an end. I think about it now with a heavy heart. The cock crow which I hear still is part of a dream world into which I retreat when things begin to get too much for me. Immediately I think of it, vistas of a long-ago land flick through my head. I am carried on my grandmother's back to be shown chicks in a coop. I sit at the farm kitchen table, smell the salt bacon frying, and look at the sun rising in the east, silhouetting the ash tree on the bank above the burn and making a golden light behind old trees long fallen into the disused rickyard. A cock crows and I carry a tea basket to the field where a labourer is using a scythe to 'open the roads' for harvest. It crows, and cocks miles away answer. I kept bees for the taste of clover honey cut from one of those ivory-white sections kept in the back porch of my grandfather's house. I kept bantams for all my yesterdays, and while the real sound gets on the nerves of some people, the remembered sound soothes mine. It takes me away up into the white, drifting clouds. I breathe the summer air and only the cry of the curlew moves me quite as much. I suppose this is hard for some people to understand. It all goes with the scent of burning logs or a peatfire, the sound of a squeaking axle and the jolting and grinding of ironshod cart wheels on a hard road.

17 TALE OF TWO BIRDS

There was a time when I kept a cock pheasant, incubated and hatched from a clutch of eggs set under one of my bantams in a specially constructed pen. It was a long term project, this raising a pheasant to imprint bantams on him in the hope that one day I might produce what I called a 'Phantom'. The experiment worked, but the resulting phantom died. All the other eggs ever produced proved infertile. In the course of my daily visits to the pen I began to encounter a robin that had discovered a way into what was otherwise a top security cage. The robin would flutter round the pen making desperate efforts to get out but, in its panic, failing to find its exit place. Then, after a week or two, it settled down. Instead of trying to avoid me it would come and perch near me, watching what I was doing with the food I had brought. Robins often show interest in what a man is doing with a fork or spade and wait for the odd worm or titbit to be uncovered. My robin, a cock bird, was ready to be hand-fed and in a short time it would fly from the perch in the pen and settle on my hand. He would take small crumbs I held between my fingers but things went beyond this little ritual. Soon he began to keep me company outside the pen, flying to catch up with me when I went to the hut to get food for free-ranging bantams and some old brown hens I had rescued from a battery. On the bleakest and wettest of winter's days the robin never failed to accompany me. He was there in the morning at first light, and there in the twilight when I went to lock up. I talked to him and he cocked his head. I held out my hand and, with or without food, he would settle on it. Sometimes he perched on my shoulder. I was fascinated and delighted. A wild bird had never come near me before. I had long been convinced that years of shooting and slaughtering game, something I abandoned and never did again after keeping pheasants and ducks, had branded me as a killer, someone to be avoided at all costs. Although I couldn't exactly aspire to be a kind of St Francis, I took satisfaction from the knowledge that this bird trusted me. I tried to make friends with other small birds. We had several pairs of hedge sparrows on our ground but they kept clear of me even when I threw food in their direction. Blackbirds never trusted me. Magpies and jays, of course, had their guilt and never trusted anyone on two legs. The robin seemed a one-off for other robins kept their distance. He, perky little bird that he was, actually saw them off from our ground, for it was his territory. All that was in it was his! One day I put a small piece of bread between my lips to see what he would do and he came and hovered in front of my face like a humming bird helping himself to the bread. This too, became a ritual. I fed him this way every day. Proud of my relationship with the robin I pointed him out to a friend who visited us.

'Do you see that small bird moving in the blackthorns?' I asked. 'It's a robin, and if I call him he will come!'

My visitor shook his head and smiled. He was certain I was pulling his leg. I called and the bird came looping down the slope, swung round my head and hovered in front of my face. It was the first time I had ever tried to call him and I don't know why I did but it worked. Thereafter I called the robin whenever I had a mind to, and he came. He roosted somewhere near the gable of the cottage and was there, like a shepherd's dog, waiting for the day to begin when I came out. This went on for three years and I often demonstrated how he responded to my call when people visited us. About this time a half wild cat came to haunt the garden beyond the kitchen window. Her relatives managed to lie in wait for a brood of young golden pheasants I was rearing and, snatching at them through the wire, murdered them one by one. I was very much against feral cats but my wife insisted in taming and encouraging this particular female which, highly strung and nervous though it was, came in through the scullery window for food. It was soon obvious that the 'wild' cat wanted a place to have a litter of kittens and, encouraged even more by my wife, had them in a shoebox cupboard next to the Aga. One of the kittens turned out to be Topsy, herself a highly-strung feline, all black but with a kind of sooty brown glow to her fur. Her mother was black and white but in her blood line there was Burmese and a trace of Siamese. Because she was the most nervous and attractive kitten in the litter Topsy won me over. When her mother, who had by this time insisted upon having a second litter, had to be put down, Topsy was adopted and the other kittens given to friends. I little thought my poor robin would one day fall prey to this huntress. Topsy felt the call of the wild strongly. Soon she began bringing us her kills, a mouse in the morning, a shrew in the afternoon, sometimes a vole in the evening. She went on to bigger and better things, a wood pigeon one day, and then a grey squirrel and a couple of stoats. I didn't mind her killing stoats or the grey squirrel, but I was bothered about the number of birds Topsy pounced on. She killed more than her share of blackbirds, thrushes, wrens, tomtits, a goldcrest or two, and then a robin. That first robin was a young bird. My 'tame' robin knew what a cat is about. He was able to detect Topsy in the snowberry bushes or the undergrowth round about, even when she made herself look like a harmless black shadow. One day, however, there was a deluge of rain and the tame robin perched in the bushes. Topsy brought him to me, dead as a doornail. I turned him over on my palm and my heart was heavy. A robin is a robin, a cat is a cat. They know one another. They live in a world that is about survival. Every day a sparrow falls and a hawk hits a wire. Every second someone is born and someone dies. I was very depressed about what had happened. I renewed efforts to encourage another robin to accept my friendship. None did.

A few weeks after the death of poor cock robin, while I was on my way up to the hens, I saw a cock pheasant on the path behind the long greenhouse. Instead of the pheasant going like an arrow into the cover of trees beyond the path he immediately hurried towards me. I stood still while it struck me that although this was a mature bird something had triggered his recollection of having been fed by a keeper. The estate-keeper's rearing ground was away on the other side of the limestone ridge behind the cottage so I doubted whether this bird was one of the current release in the covers. It seemed more likely he had come from woodland below us and had been there at least a year, for he was a mature bird. The seemingly tame pheasant picked up the pellets I scattered for him and behaved like a domestic fowl. I was delighted. The following day he showed up again while I was feeding the hens. He was actually more nervous of the cockerels in the flock than he was of me. When the cockerels threatened him he fluffed himself out until he looked at least twice his size and they were daunted by this encounter. I fed my birds twice a day. Sometimes the cock pheasant wandered and missed a meal, but gradually he seemed to get into the feeding routine and was there for his ration whenever food was scattered. I talked to him. Like the robin, he would put his head on one side as though trying to understand what I was saying. I began to feed him from my hand. One or two of the tamer bantams would join in and sometimes they all jostled to get the pellets on my palm. I was as proud of this relationship as I had been of that with the robin. The handsome black-necked pheasant was a big bird with well-grown spurs and saw off any other pheasant that happened to come over our wall. None of these intruders was in the least tame. The moment they saw me, if they weren't already on the run, they took to the air and flew back the way they had come. Soon I began to call the cock pheasant to me. None of my bantams was more tame. I felt that if I had wanted to, I could have picked him up and carried him.

At about this time my wife adopted two yelping, loud-voiced seagulls that had nested somewhere up on the cliff. The gulls came each morning for a handout and made a noise until they were fed. Some mornings they paddled on the flat top of our dormer windows. I was forced to get out of bed and see them off but they always came back again. I sometimes gave them bread, but my wife gave them cake and digestive biscuits. Occasionally one of them bolted a whole biscuit and the biscuit distended the bird's throat before it finally crumbled. It seemed to me a manufacturer of digestive biscuits could make a commercial about gulls and their liking for digestive biscuits and I mentioned this in my weekly piece in *Country Life*. Shortly afterwards I had a letter from the Chairman of United Biscuits, Sir Hector Laing, who told me he was sending me a few biscuits for my gulls. I thanked him promising to call the gulls McVitie or Crawford. The biscuits arrived in due course, a large carton of them, but on the day after the North Wales representatives of United Biscuits brought their rations the gulls disappeared! A great gale drove them away and they stayed away. By this time the black-necked pheasant had started to come round the door. He was offered biscuits, first one, and then two. He loved them and came for two in the morning and two in the afternoon. He would devour every crumb but two biscuits were his limit. If we put down three one was always left. I wrote to Sir Hector explaining what I had done and saying that I would now name the pheasant McVitie. Sir Hector wrote back and gave his blessing. Later he telephoned to say he was sending McVitie a few more biscuits for he had caught up with the saga of our black-necked pheasant when he picked up a *Country Life* while flying to America by Concord. With such a generous patron McVitie couldn't help but thrive. His plumage acquired an even finer sheen. I took some colour pictures of him and sent one to Sir Hector to show him McVitie was really worthy of his name.

McVitie went over the wall soon after this and didn't come back. I looked everywhere for him but couldn't find him. I thought some local villain had way-laid him in the lane, or lured him with his favourite biscuit. Perhaps, I told myself, one of those foreign waiters working from the local hotels had shot him for I had actually seen one of these characters, walking down the main street (in the middle of the day) with a shotgun under his arm, and a pheasant dangling from his hand! Perhaps his very boldness saved him. No one called the Police. I thought to tell the gamekeeper about McVitie. He said he would look out for him, but one cock pheasant looked very like another. When the shooting season began His Lordship was hardly likely to agree that one of the birds getting up before the guns of his guests was mine and not his, but he might just thank me for fattening it for him! I despaired of seeing McVitie again, but I might have guessed what it was about. Just like domestic fowl, pheasants undergo the moult. McVitie was away, skulking in the undergrowth while his fine new feathers grew. One day there he was, back outside the kitchen window, looking expectant, waiting for his digestive biscuits. He didn't leave us all winter. This was a great relief particularly as the time for the cock shoot arrived and I heard the farmers accompanying the keepers banging off along the hedge sides and among the thickets near our boundary. McVitie was aware of the danger. He kept away from the area. We went on into spring. I decided he was in his third year, judging from the length of his spurs and I am sure he was. How long does a wild pheasant survive, I wonder? It has enemies, including dogs, cats and the stoat.

Friends who came and met McVitie said he would look grand on a plate with a bottle of red wine at hand. They couldn't believe that someone who had shot thousands of birds spared this one. I shook my head. Such things were behind me and I didn't want to be reminded of my mindlessness.

McVitie had become more and more tame. Sometimes when he hurried down from the little orchard to the small garden area beyond the kitchen window, and no one handed him the biscuits, he would fly up onto the window sill and look round the scullery, flapping down to get his breakfast when it was thrown onto the garden. On other occasions he would stand patiently waiting for the back door to be opened and I would go out and he would feed from my hand. His relationship with Topsy was one of mutual respect. He wasn't afraid of her and she was perhaps just a little wary of him. She was jealous of my conversation with him and always hung about looking rather abject while I fed him. When with his throat and crop bulging with food, McVitie stood a while to let his meal go down, Topsy sat like a doorstopper. She didn't approve of his walking into the kitchen, which he sometimes did, whether we were there or not, leaving his footprints on the floor. I must say McVitie looked magnificent when he was over the moult. After the first dismaying absence, which lasted perhaps six weeks in all, he stayed away the next year at the same time and I suffered the same anxiety every time I heard a gunshot. I knew an idle character who might stalk my very tame bird to make an end of him. People going up the footpath admired him and wondered at his lack of fear but it was a strange thing that McVitie was not really at ease even with me outside our ground. He would run into the bushes if anyone appeared on the stile or the footpath. I was reassured by this but there was just a chance that someone might kill him.

He came back after what must have been his third moult and stayed right through the shooting season. In the spring he called up a harem of hen pheasants who picked their way over our two orchards with him until I came near. McVitie didn't run, but his ladies would bolt, or fly like rockets up and over the trees. They always came back again in a little while for he was probably the finest male bird for miles. One of his wives nested at the bottom of the hedge. I discovered the nest when a bantam began laying there too, but the wild pheasant wasn't in favour of shared premises and gave up. A magpie took the entire clutch in an hour that morning. If he hadn't McVitie the second might have hatched in his father's territory.

McVitie not only approached kitchen and scullery windows for his meals, and waited for me at the back door, but at times he came across the court and knocked on the French windows. I would go and get him his biscuits but I was never quite sure about this knocking. Was he asking for biscuits or seeing a rival in the reflection of the window pane? When I got up from my chair he would leave the French windows and dash across the court to the back door. We always exchanged the time of day. He would cluck and croon when I talked to him. My wife and I regularly asked one another, 'Has he been this morning? Did you leave his biscuits out?' If we went anywhere for a day we always made sure his biscuits, sometimes three, were left on the flowerbed by the side of the court. McVitie knew where to go. Sometimes a grey squirrel came upon the treat and McVitie went hungry. If this happened he always hung about until we came back. I once saw him make a frantic dash at a squirrel that tried to take the biscuit and Topsy who had a thing about squirrels, raced after the little grey squirrel, sending it back up the trunk of the tree at top speed.

In his fourth year with us McVitie was accompanied by a young, ring-necked pheasant, a bird that flapped over our wall after one of the shoots. It limped badly and wasn't very strong on the wing. To save the injured bird I caught him up and penned him in a bantam run. When his internment was at an end the ring-neck quickly flew over our high, wych elm hedge to pastures new but soon he had come back. Although McVitie saw off every other bird that ventured down on his side of the wall he tolerated this young one. They walked the grass together. The ring-neck fed on the fringe of the bantam flock but rarely accompanied the older bird when he came for biscuits. I was greatly intrigued by this relationship. Looking at it in an anthropomorphic way, I saw it as something paternal, but in the course of time the ring-neck left to gather himself a few hens and McVitie had the place to himself again.

In his fifth year McVitie was looking his age a little and one day I noticed him skulking in the hedge bottom, bedraggled and wet. I was afraid he had contracted a chill. When he came to be fed he wheezed and made a piping noise. He took a long time to eat his biscuits and stayed closer at hand. He was slow to go up to roost in the pines where he had always had favourite perching places used for one night at a time in sequence. Perhaps there was greater safety in this? I worried about him now and one morning I picked him up and took him into our long greenhouse where he would be warmer and able to keep dry. He did seem to get a little better but the piping noise continued. I think now I should have taken him to the vet. He rallied every so often and ate the biscuits and mixed corn and pellets, but nothing lives forever, I told myself, and McVitie had had a good life. Then one morning when I went to give him his biscuits I found him dead. I could have cried. His plumage was in absolutely perfect condition, but his body had wasted underneath it all. Poor old fellow, he was done with flapping his wings and challenging rivals, done with telling us when he was going up to roost or sounding off from a limb of one of his favourite trees. I buried him with as much sorrow as I had buried my dog. I knew that bird. It shared my time along with other living creatures. That means something when we only live once.

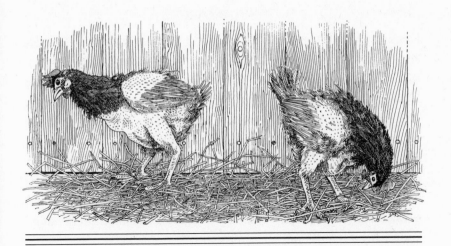

18 A FINAL WORD ON
THE CHICKEN AND THE EGG

If I say there is a price to be paid for everything I am using a platitude but I may be talking about the price of peace and the price of war, or something everyday and elementary, like the price of a breakfast egg. Yet there is a major moral issue even in this – the price of conscience over a barbarity that degrades the person who knows how the egg was produced just as much as it degrades the man who makes use of the wretched bird, keeping it in a small wire cage that wears away its neck and breast feathers and encourages its unused toes to grow and hook themselves round the mesh beneath. While this is happening the bird's leg muscles are atrophying and it ceases to be able to stand up. But then it isn't intended to waste its time standing up. It is supposed to be laying an egg a day. When its record card shows that it isn't it is dragged free of the mesh its overgrown toenails have been hooked round, strung up by the head or the heels, passed round a kind of gantry where its neck is drawn, its feathers whipped off and its naked corpse presented for evisceration. It is then broiled to make chicken in the basket or

Kentucky Fried, that finger-licking treat advertised all over America and Britain. Emotive words these, about the egg we are supposed to go to work on. We need to go to work on something. We have to eat to live. Eating is not a minority habit but if they want an egg from the miserable bird that spends its life in a prison cell they will probably say they don't care where the egg comes from or how it gets there so long as it is there. They are hungry. They leave the means to the minority. The minority put the egg in the supermarket. They, the majority, would complain bitterly and perhaps over-turn the government, if called on to pay substantially more for their egg. I say this in case someone thinks I don't know what it is all about.

I have thought about it over and over again since I took some battery birds to stay overnight in my old hen-house to meet their end in my deep freeze, a dozen or so birds I thought would make tasty dinners. I come of farming stock so perhaps I should take the practical view point a man who makes his living exploiting animals must adopt. (It is surely a better thing I think to exploit a chicken or a bullock than to grind the faces of the poor or see them slaughtered in order to make a million?) I didn't know that I was this kind of soft-centred sentimentalist, until I had to decide about the wretched hens from the battery. I often used to smile when my poor old aunts went about wailing and burying their heads in their aprons after the contractor came to take away the young pigs they had been fattening; I didn't appreciate that they had looked into the eyes of those piglets and knew them, but how can anyone look at a hen and know it for anything but a bird-brained creature? I had bundled my hens into the old hen-house and shut the door on them on the dark night I brought them home. I had seen them in the subdued light of their galleried prison, each one 'banged' up, not just for the night, but until fate might intervene and they took the 'long walk' to a chicken gallows. The horror of that scene did make a certain impact upon me as the man from whom I was buying my chicken dinners pulled the brown

[162]

hens from their cages and popped them into the sack. And there was the atmosphere of the place, the dust, the eerie light, the unnatural appearance of hundreds of scrawny, neck-naked chickens with heads sticking from each compartment, the movement of that feeder and the odd egg rolling gently down to the barrier as the imprisoned hen dutifully did her bit. This was forever, so far as those production line birds were concerned. Not for them the bright sunlight, the springy green turf, the wind ruffling their brown feathers; but this is not to say their eyes were dull. Their eyes were bright. They crooned every so often. Occasionally one of them cackled like any free-range hen that has laid away in the long grass. They had fresh water and food. Even their droppings were hygenically disposed of to make fertilizer. It was just my inbuilt anthropomorphism, and I managed to overcome these feelings when I was handed my sacks tied at the neck with baler twine. I put the sacks in the boot of my car. When I arrived at the hen-house I undid the twine and tipped the birds gently onto the floor, not waiting to see how they settled for they were content to rest on the grass I had spread in the hen-house before going to get them.

To some people a hen is a bird, but an egg comes from a crate. A steak is something quite remote from the young bullock swinging his tail and galloping over the meadow to escape the flies. Milk for the average townee comes from a bottle. A cow has very little to do with it. Does anyone think of a cow while he pours cream into coffee? My battery hens were chicken dinners! I went to bed more concerned about how I would pluck them and prepare them for the freezer than about their escape from prison. They weren't intended to survive. I hadn't thought about rehabilitation. I knew that an elderly hen had more flavour than a young one, but I had no intention of feeding them until they were two or three years old and needed to be parboiled. Dear me, I thought, I have hours of feather-plucking before me as well as the unpleasant task of drawing and dressing those brown birds.

It was a bright, crisp autumn morning when I went up to the old hen-house to inspect my chicken dinners. One, alas, had jumped the gun and died. Its wasted joints had parted and it had come down on its keel bone, dislocating both legs. It hadn't survived long. Another poor bird had to be lifted aside. It couldn't get out of the crouching posture its body had been in for nearly a year. Two birds were on their feet but leaning on the woodwork like town loungers. They couldn't possibly stand without propping themselves against something. All of these half-naked birds looked at me hopefully, blinking in the unusually strong morning sunlight. They clucked and crooned. Their apparent friendliness touched me. No, I told myself, they weren't chicken dinners! They were alive and they must continue to live! I brought water and fed them for I had pellets in store. I was afraid of them venturing out in case, being unused to a cold atmosphere, they caught chills. I put a wire netting door on the hen-house so that the fresh air could get to them. I looked them over and sighed at their pathetic state. A bird with its feathers worn off from head to keel bone, and feet curled up like those of a donkey whose hooves have been neglected is a most sorry sight. Those that tried to get about looked as though they had been at the gin and were the worse for it. I thought I was lucky not to have lost more. I buried the first casualty and made up my mind there would be no more if I could possibly prevent it.

When I kept sheep I undoubtedly made the mistake of looking the foolish creatures in the eye. It is comparatively easy to contemplate killing a creature one doesn't know. Even the man with his finger on the button has this great advantage of being able to stay detached. A fighter pilot doesn't really have a human enemy. He has a target. Humanity is a great weakness in man, a cynic will tell you. I made my mistake when I knew a lamb to be a living creature. Those unfortunate hens huddled in the hen-house, looked to me to restore them to their personal comfort, even, perhaps, to return them to the warm battery. I couldn't make them quite so comfortable, but I could, given time, let them discover the world as it should have been for them when they began to lay the one brown egg a day the slavemaster demanded of them. It is imposs- ible to give an account of what happened fourteen or fifteen years ago without being a little emotional about it for I was a prisoner of my emotions. From thinking that these brown hens were mine, bought and paid for, I had a duty to them. They were in my hands. I couldn't kill them. I had to save them. I suppose I had come to this rather late in the day. Other people might testify to a spiritual experience that persuaded them to adopt a particular faith, to make a stand and declare their conviction. I didn't really appreciate it, but I was on the way to the conviction that all life, not just human life, but all life, is sacred. The commandment Thou shalt not kill, like most other so-called divine commandments, has never been collectively honoured. Even those who refuse to kill raise little protest against those who insist upon doing their killing for them. I had a long way to go. I would even yet cull a dozen bantam cockerels, but those battery hens, I promised, would live until they died of natural causes, if they never laid another egg!

Well, in time their feathers grew. In time, with a little encourage- ment, they ventured out onto the grass. They proved more tame than any domestic fowl I have ever known. They ambled after me, clucking and crooning and feeding round my feet. They were heavy-built hens of a special laying strain, but of course they not only had a moult coming up, they had to recover from it before any of them would lay. My affection for them increased the longer I had them. I would stand and watch them when they came running to be fed, moving like bundly old ladies running to catch a bus. They loved company. It was obvious they loved their new found freedom. No poultry-keeper would have fed them for as long as I did without thought of return, but then one day one of them laid an egg. She was a bird now in shining plumage and with a bright red comb, a sure sign that a hen is ready to lay. I looked at the shine on the other birds. They were all looking wonderful. They all began to lay! Six months after being on the production-line they were completely recovered from the moult and in tip-top condition. I was very proud of them.

After the initial loss there were no more casualties. Each of those birds which, had things taken their normal course after their failure to meet their target as battery hens, would have been destroyed laid almost three hundred eggs in the next eleven months. They made a nonsense of the control employed by the battery-keeper. They were certainly not kept in perpetual light and weren't in a temperature-controlled atmosphere. They were allowed to go out in the rain and they often did. They picked up insects from the grass and cleared the bushes of caterpillars. They lumbered in pursuit of flies the way my smaller and much lighter bantams did. They came to another moult and stopped laying but were not under threat of execution. I never asked myself how much the moult was costing or thought about how long 'infertility' would last. In their own good time they began to lay their large brown eggs again. The yolks of those healthy eggs were a strong yellow and they made wonderful cakes and omelettes. It seems to me battery hens are kept in cages because it is cheaper in terms of man hours to keep them immobile. No one has to hunt for eggs. Their keeper fills the hopper at the end of the conveyor belt and looks to his thermostat. The dimmed lights stay dim. It is a world of half-light on the road to hell and no cock ever crows. There is no daybreak in the dusty upper reaches of these Sing Sing buildings in which spiders weave their webs and flies became entangled in them. The spiders devour the flies while down below man whose job it is peers at his record cards. He never lets his inmates go before the parole board. There is no such thing as parole. The prisoner will never see the outside world and is thoroughly institutionalised. Only a sentimentalist weeps about what happens. Can a bird imagine anything? Does it know what is natural and what is unnatural? Does the pig living indoors in similar conditions, his small pen sluiced and his pink body haloed with fine golden hair, know anything about the outside world in which his mud-blackened, unpedigreed relative lives? Would all pigs do better without a balanced diet of special mix, an injection of antibiotic and, a dose of hormones? There is quite a difference between bacon and eggs of course. The egg is easier to obtain and costs less per pound, but make no mistake, the consumer pays for the prison and the special food. Indirectly he is responsible for the whole business. The battery owner insists that he only satisfies the consumer's demand for a breakfast egg. If the customer must have a conscience about the egg he can go and buy free-range. Some farmers actually go to the super market, buy the battery egg and take it home to apply a little honest mud to the shell before they sell it as free-range. They know the fads of the public. The battery man has taken advice and feeds what is needed to make a pale yolk into a bright yellow one. He wouldn't keep hens that lay white-shelled eggs in his cages. No one in his right mind keeps birds that lay eggs of the wrong colour even if the colour of the shell has nothing to do with its content. The public are fools and their folly is something to be exploited.

I won't say I felt strongly about any of this at the time. I was satisfied with the rehabilitation of those brown hens. I developed a warm affection for them. They were great old birds. I was interested to discover just how long they would live and how many years they would keep on laying. The economics of the thing wouldn't have pleased an accountant who would draw dividing lines and work out all the opportunities for profit. I had missed the very first bonus. It was like selling shares without taking a dividend! I could have sold my brown hens to a restaurateur and he could have served them up as chicken kiev or something exotic with tasty sauce and special herbs and made a handsome profit. I didn't and immediately contracted a loss, going into the red when I let them recover from the moult without wringing their necks. I didn't cost it out because there was no profit from the sale of eggs. I ate the eggs or gave a dozen or two to friends. Such folly would have put me up before the Board had I been the servant of a company! Profit is what the system is about and I was flouting the basic law of capitalism, being a sort of Don Quixote saving hens from a fate they richly deserved. The brown hens went on and on. Most of them lived to reach the age of six or seven but then one or two, whose old bones were perhaps becoming more arthritic through under-use in the early stage of growth, fell by the wayside. They simply settled down on the floor of the hen-house, let their heads droop and died like old, worn-out workers. A few ceased to lay but toddled on, obviously soon to be geriatric. One or two looked as good as ever and lived for seven or eight years but the weather, the hard winters and their declining ability to scrape and scratch, whittled the old ones down to two or three. By the tenth year only one survived. She, believe it or not, would come into lay in late spring and lay a couple of dozen brown eggs before giving up. We didn't use these eggs on account of the hen's great age. She went on to reach the age of fourteen. She got slow in coming down from the hen-house of a morning and was shaky like an elderly relative who should really have been put in a home. I was no less fond of this aged bird. She reminded me of that day when I toured the battery witnessing the cull. She had cost me ten shillings – fifty new pence. She had rewarded me with many hundreds of eggs and I tried to make her declining years as comfortable as possible. As one of my Welsh freinds might have said, there's sentimentality for you! I am not ashamed of being a sentimentalist. A man without a degree of feeling is inhuman. The proper place for him is in a cage.

The very last of my birds died of extreme old age. I didn't think to rescue other birds from the prison and death row. Maybe I should have done, but where would it end, I asked myself? Could I buy the freedom of thousands upon thousands of birds supplying breakfast eggs to a multitude of people? Cruelty is inherent in human existence and inseparable, some people would say, from survival. I buried the old biddy. She was painfully thin, the fine condition of her feathers was long gone. She weighed nothing. I put her well down in case the dog dug her up.

This has been a book about the birds in my life. I am not equipped to discuss philosophy or offer anything but my homespun, and not very profound, theories to explain my being here. Even the greatest philosopher can't really say why we are here or where we are going. We are here, encroaching upon one another, hating, loving, creating and destroying. One man sees the mud and another the stars, someone has observed. One man believes in mankind and another knows that collectively man is the worst animal of all, the one that makes war against his own kind and stands callously watching the weak and helpless being slaughtered, mortared and bombed off the face of the earth. A person such as myself, with no faith in politicians or ministers of religion, turns back to the innocent and harmless creatures that share his world. It is anthropomorphic to see a mirror for human behaviour in the way birds behave but a hen cackles in the undergrowth and the cockerel hurries to escort her back out of the jungle. Food is scattered and the male bird clucks and draws the attention of the females to the special titbits he is discovering. He encourages them to eat what he has found and actually drops it for them. The human male couldn't behave any better and often doesn't behave as well! An unfortunate bird becomes unwell and is perhaps first shunned and then killed (put out of its misery) by other members of the flock. A bantam takes it into its head to spring into the air and fly like a crow crossing the field and other hens immediately scold her. A hen with chicks joins the feeding flock and the youngsters are allowed to feed before birds that are ravenously hungry, for the young must be given an opportunity to improve. As in human society, there is a hierarchy – a pecking order – and newcomers must learn their place in the community they have joined. The old cock crows and the young cock learns.

A philosopher must surely take account of the fact that even he has limited contact with his world, that he was born part of a pattern, sharing his world with certain people, a few animals and birds perhaps, a fortuitous or disastrous thing, which he must make his mind up about when he makes a pronouncement about the whole meaning of man's existence. I am afraid I have no conclusion. I will die without knowing why I was put down where I was and had the particular contacts I have had both with men and the creatures that share my time and place. But then I doubt whether the purpose of my being is to discover who I am, but rather to live until I die, and to do both as well as I am able.